FAMILY MATTERS

One family, two wars…

Janet H. Robinson

Read Fox Books

1st edition published in 2016
by Read Fox books

All rights reserved © Janet H. Robinson 2016

No part of this publication may be reproduced, stored in a retrieval system, or transmitted in any form or any mean, electronic, mechanical, photocopy, recoding or otherwise without prior written consent from the copyright holder.

The rights of Janet Robinson to be identified as author of this work has been asserted in accordance with Section 77 of the Copyright, designs and Patents Act 1988

ISBN 978-0-993256417-9

Distributed by the author, 16 The Meadows,
Hay on Wye, Hereford HR3 5LF

Email: janethoperobinson@gmail.com

Printed in the United Kingdom
By Powerprint
Oxford Chambers
High Street
Llandrindod Wells
Powys, LD1 6AG

Acknowledgements

As this is a personal memoir there has been little primary research other than delving into the Census Records – a search now made so much easier through the internet. Gone are the days when family history research required visits to London and the handling of heavy volumes in St Katharine's House.

I am very grateful to Brian Lawrence who has allowed me to quote from his excellent book: *Hatfield at War* (Hatfield Local History Society. Revised Edition 2016). The same society has allowed me to use material from my own *The Tingey's of Hatfield* assembled by Frank Cox in 2000. I found interesting and useful details in *Fleetville: A community in St Albans* (St. Albans Museum Service 2009). I have referred to *Hatfield and its People* – that bible of Hatfield's local history - published between 1959-64 by the WEA under the guidance of Lionel Munby. Jenny Sherwood of Hemel Hempstead Local History society was most helpful with regard to the Baldry family. I also acknowledge use of Wikipedia for some background material.

The picture of St Albans Road in Ch.5 is reproduced with permission from a Frith postcard. All other photographs are from our family albums.

I trust that the owners of the houses mentioned which still exist will forgive the historic descriptions of them.

Above all I am greatly indebted to both my parents for their substantial and lively contributions to this text. Sadly they are not here to be thanked in person but much of the impetus to write this memoir has been to provide a platform for their work.

Both my niece, Hilary Tagg and Mark, my husband, have kindly commented and proof read my several drafts.

And, of course, the warmest acknowledgement is to my family, one of whom has suffered burnt suppers and frequent neglect during the composition of this memoir. Without them, of course, I would not have written it.

Locations

I have tried without success to draw a sketch map of the Hatfield I knew. The roads are now so buried or distorted beneath the New Town of the 1950s that I can only – for those to whom it matters – give a rough approximation of the places I mention.

Chapter 2: Mrs. Payne and the girls walked from Nast Hyde, and eventually into Roe Green Lane and up into St Albans Road.

Chapter 3: "Newtown" ran roughly from where Wellfield Road crosses into the B197 - which was French Horn Lane, to where Lemsford Road crossed to Briar's Lane. The Right of Ways joined St Albans Road to the Common.

Tingey's first shop and 101 were both in St Albans Road west of White Lion Square.

The Fiddle pub stood at the corner where Fiddlebridge Lane joins Roe Green Lane.

Chantry Lane still exists though its course is somewhat altered.

Countess Anne's school (which had become a Church of England Infants' School) was by 1913 in the Great North Road south of the roundabout near the Broadway.

Dagmar School was on the old Great North Road, north of the Old Hertford Road.

Introduction

There were not many papers, cards and leaflets to sort through after my mother died. She was an organised person and by the time she had made two moves from the family house she had whittled down her memorabilia, and that of her husband and my father, Randall, to a couple of boxes and some photograph albums. Fragments of my grandparents' lives are mixed with them and I know less of their history.

I riffled through a box. There were three old children's books and a blazer badge of my first school, Newtown House – items over twenty five years apart in my mother's life. There was a packet of her metal badges and medals won for service in the Red Cross during the World War II and certificates saying that she, Mrs Florence Tingey, had passed examinations in First Aid and Home Nursing.

I picked up an old exercise book, its cover long lost, the pages alternating between ruled and squared paper. The date on the first page is October 1921 so my mother was eleven when she wrote very tidily in pencil how to knit a baby's sock and following that there are instructions and neat diagrams for making Baby's nightgown and Barrow Coat. What is a barrow coat? And on the back page, surprisingly, there was a diagram of a netball pitch with names of the players placed in their positions.

Some letters and cards were grouped and tied with ribbon: "Letters after Randall's death". Then there was a packet full of handmade birthday cards from our daughters, Kate and Nell; cards made by my brother and me and a reminder of my own Gran: *To Florrie from her loving mother*.

In another box she had kept some diaries and papers of my father. There is a leather notebook inscribed inside the front cover *From Mother to Randall, Xmas 1920*. In it he had recorded football and cricket scores. Like her too, he wrote down some memories of his childhood, kept photos of football teams, motorcycles and cars he had possessed. And there were a number of record cards where, urged by me, my father in his retirement had jotted down memories of people and places in an attempt to put together a family history.

The keepsakes were reminders for both of them – souvenirs of significant events and moments of happiness and sorrow. Yet, many are also part of my memories for they tell me stories of their childhoods and of their parents which have been woven into the warp of my life. The threads are sometimes faded and broken. In parts I expect I have embroidered over the weave. Some of my own early experiences were pictured for me by my mother and I cannot always be sure if the pictures are entirely mine. But that is inevitable. There are, as Herodotus said "infinite renderings of the past".

I know little about my grandparents' childhood and I know more about my father's family history than that of my mother. To fill in the gaps and perhaps find some secrets I have consulted the Census and old directories for I did not ask enough questions. I will not travel far into the past. Once the leaves on the family tree are inscribed only with names I am less interested. It is the stories and idiosyncrasies of one's forebears and the family traits that link the generations that fascinate me. Everything gets lost so easily and I want to capture what I can.

Because I have been extraordinarily lucky, families matter to me and this story is about mine.

Chapter 1

Bedtime Stories

"Drat!" exclaimed Gran. Laying aside her knitting she snatched my bath towel from the top of the closed stove as the scent of toasted cotton rose into the air. I, happily playing with a yellow duck in the papier maché bath on the hearthrug, had not noticed.

"No real harm done, thank goodness," said Gran examining a slight scorch mark on the towel, "Now out you come and I'll read you a story."

Drying me carefully she dusted me down with talcum powder and helped me into my striped flannelette pyjamas and red woolly dressing gown. I moved my three legged stool close to her armchair and she opened my chosen book and began to read. "Once upon a time there were four little rabbits…" All too soon her voice would drop gently to a close: "But Flopsy, Mopsy and Cotton-tail had bread and milk and blackberries for supper".[1]

I knew I would get no more stories that night but I was drowsy and content. Gran lightened the weight of the bath by scooping up a bucketful of water and taking it into the kitchen. Then she returned and carried the bath away. Our cats, Pooh and Jim, who had been waiting under the dining room table, quickly emerged and curled up together in front of the stove.

Many evenings in my early childhood were like this. This particular memory must be embedded in the months of the phoney war from the autumn of 1939 until April the following year before the bombing began. My widowed grandmother had come to live with us because my parents did not want her to endure the war alone.

---

[1] Beatrix Potter: The Tale of Peter Rabbit – this and brief mentions of other tales were published by Frederick Warne between 1902 and 1930

I thought of her as a lookalike Mrs. Tiggy-winkle without the prickles[2], for she was short, round, smelled of lavender and wore navy blue patterned dresses covered with an enveloping apron. In the afternoons the apron would be exchanged for a hand-knitted cardigan with a folded handkerchief stuck in the pocket. If she was going to St Albans on the bus she would ritually change into clean underwear just in case she had an accident and had to go to hospital. Her grey hair, still streaked with black, was plaited and she would wind it into a small, neat bun at the back and secure it with hair pins. She used to brush it out at night, comb the loose hairs out of the brush, wind them round her finger and toss them out of the window. My father, once discovering a chaffinch nest which had fallen out of the garden hedge, brought it into the kitchen to show us. It was partially lined with ring-sized soft twists of Gran's hair.

Since my mother was much employed in the office of our shop by day and engaged in Red Cross work on many evenings, Gran Hope added many valuable contributions to the household. She was a conscientious wielder of dusters, saved tea leaves to sprinkle on the carpet and brush vigorously to remove dirt; polished furniture and peeled vegetables. Besides reading me stories she tried in vain to teach me to knit. Large wooden needles were bought and a ball of rainbow wool. It was a thankless task for I am left-handed – and cack-handed - and I could not get the knack. The indignity of having the wool cut off the needles wiped out any wish to continue. I was soon relegated to holding skeins of wool for Gran to wind; a pleasant occupation as one learned to flick one's thumbs out of the way as the wool flowed by.

She was always busy with her knitting but sometimes of an evening her hands would droop onto her lap and my father would tease her for dozing. "I'm just resting my eyes" she would say with dignity. She was a cheerful, gentle little soul but

---

[2] In Beatrix Potter's story Mrs. Tiggy-winkle is a hedgehog.

not lacking character. "Drat the cat!" she would say with spirit when one of ours almost tripped her up, "Drat" being her worst expletive. Being thoughtful and self-effacing, she always retired early to her bedroom wanting to give my parents time to themselves. Gran stayed with us until she died in 1962 aged 87 and, by then, not in her "perfect mind".

Did she read stories to my mother in the kitchen of their little house in St Albans during the First World War? Did they sit beside the polished black-leaded grate on which a kettle purred? My mother told me that the copper in the scullery was lit to boil the water on Saturday nights, the tin bath taken off a hook on the wall and lugged upstairs to the biggest bedroom where a fire had been lit. The water was carried up in large jugs and no doubt everyone in the house took turns. My mother could not enjoy so often my experience of soporific warmth.

I never asked either of them if they shared stories at bedtime. My grandmother may well have read *Dollytown* aloud. That book remains amongst my mother's papers, secured in a flat box labelled "Florrie's Book: First World War".

The soft cover is creased and battered and it contains bright coloured pictures and black and white drawings inexpertly coloured by Florrie herself. Written in simple verse, it is a story about two children. Though it could be dismissed as hopelessly old fashioned, it is a wonderful fusion of reality and make-believe. Polly's doll is dropped on its head by her brother and is badly cracked. Having put

the doll to bed Polly decides with admirable practicality that:

"Some secotine and glue
Would make her quite as good as new."

That same mingling of fact and fancy reminds me that Nell, our younger daughter, once said fiercely about Sabu, her black doll: "He is so naughty that I'd smack him if I wasn't afraid of breaking his china head!" In *Dollytown* Polly and her brother play splendid imaginary games, making a coach and horses out of two dining room chairs. Such games were a part of my mother's childhood.

Reading to my children was one of great joys of being a parent. I don't know how much pleasure our elder daughter Kate had from being read Beatrix Potter when she was just two years old. But I enjoyed reading them. Indeed, sometimes I read them too dramatically. For several months I had to omit the page: "But round the end of a cucumber frame, whom should he meet but ... Mr. McGregor!!"

And, though reading *Lyle, Lyle the Crocodile* palled after reading it for ten consecutive evenings, it was still an enormous sensuous pleasure sitting there by the fire with a child on one's lap. I suspect it is unlikely that my grandmother as a child was read many stories by her mother. Life then was too hard.

Gran Hope, christened Annie Maria Baldry, was born on 19th April, 1875. My mother used to try to find some primroses to celebrate the birthday for it is also Primrose Day. I was told many times that she was the second daughter of Robert Baldry, a butler. However, it is wise to check family stories thoroughly for I know they can be embroidered, half-forgotten or are even deliberately untrue. I found in the census that Robert was born around 1843 in Barwick, Norfolk, and his father was a gamekeeper. By the 1860s his family was living in Great Gaddesden near Hemel Hempstead, Hertfordshire and two of his brothers had also become gamekeepers. Apparently Robert left home before he was eighteen and he is listed in the 1861 census as a footman in the house of William Reid, a wealthy brewer who lived at The Node in Codicote, Hertfordshire. There is Robert's name on the smudgy page of the entry, one of a long list of servants: three butlers, three footmen, two coachmen, two grooms, a governess, housekeeper, cook, two lady's maids, three housemaids, a schoolroom maid, a nurse and a kitchen maid. Imagine being the poor young girl at the bottom of that pile!

In 1868 Robert married Rosetta Mary Byrne from Hemel Hempstead by licence in St Mark's, Islington. They were probably staying at the house of her grandparents because by that time Rosetta's mother was a widow. Three years later Robert was butler to Sir Astley Paston-Cooper whose estate was Gadebridge in Hemel Hempstead.

The family lived in the Round House, which was a cottage for the accommodation of employees. Looking at the photograph kept by my grandmother the cottage was not so much round as octagonal – known by locals as the Three'penny bit cottage – covered in ivy with a single storey lean-to building on the side and surrounded by a wire fence.

By 1871 Robert and Rosetta had produced a son, named after his father. The staff at Gadebridge were less numerous than at The Node but Robert was the senior servant presiding over a footman, housekeeper, cook, one lady's maid, two housemaids and two kitchen maids. And there was a nurse, a governess and a coachman.

Robert probably earned at least £40 per annum. This may not sound much but he received all his food, a rent free house, free uniform and certain perks. Considering a skilled labourer might earn £20 p.a. without any extras it made the family moderately comfortable. It was quite unusual for a butler to be married for employers considered that a man with wife and family might spend too much time looking after them. He might even be tempted to secrete food for the children or a half-bottle of wine for a sick wife. Robert was also quite young to be a butler for in 1871 he was only twenty-eight years old.

By 1875 the family, now including two year old Alice, had moved to Kent where Robert was butler to William Waring of Woodlands, Chelsfield. This is where Annie Maria was born. By 1877 the birth of the next daughter, Florence Maud, was registered at Godmanchester in Huntingdon. The family had returned to Hemel Hempstead by January 1880 because the birth of their youngest daughter Daisy Mabel was registered there. I wonder about these frequent changes of job. Was he fussy or didn't he suit? Bearing in mind the end of his story, perhaps he drank too much. I do know that servants moved quite frequently in those days but it could not have been easy shifting your household goods and your family in a carrier's cart and, perhaps the railway from Hertfordshire to Kent then up to Huntingdon and back to Hemel Hempstead all within the space of five years.

In 1881 they were living in a cottage at Piccotts End to the north of Hemel Hempstead. One possible clue for the family's reappearance in Hertfordshire is that Rosetta's mother, described in the census as an invalid, was living with them and that may have been the reason for their return. She, Mary Ann Byrne, my great-great grandmother, is little more than a name to me. On the wall of my mother's bedroom hung a framed text beautifully embroidered on thick perforated paper[3] in shades of red, green and gold which says solemnly "In God is our Strength" This was worked by Mary Ann. And that is all we have of her.

On the 8th August 1882, catastrophe struck the Baldry family. This is the anecdote that I was told by my grandmother:

> Father was butler to Sir Astley Paston Cooper but he was killed crossing the railway.

The impression the story gives was that it was pure carelessness – possibly crossing the line in the dark, perhaps tripping over a sleeper. Would I have learned more had I asked? Or was that all Gran had been told? Did that brief explanation hide something more? Curious, I sent for a copy of Robert's death certificate:
Found dead on the London & North Western Railway with injuries calculated to show that he had been knocked down and killed by a train passing on the line.

That tallied with Gran's story but the certificate stated that Robert was not a butler but "a waiter." The inquest was held on the same day and the certificate was received from the coroner with a verdict of "Accidental death." It seemed hasty and no member of the family reported it or was mentioned. Had he come down in the world? Sometimes a railway accident can hide suicide. Had he become depressed, or alcoholic, lost his

---

[3] The thick perforated paper was introduced in the 1820s/30s and the Victorians liked using it for bookmarks and mottoes such as Rosetta's.

more prestigious job, couldn't stand his mother in law? I thought it unlikely that I would ever know.

However, recently a report of the inquest was put online[4] It tells in forensic detail of the finding of the body on the line by an engine driver, the process by which the body was taken to a local inn, the state of the corpse and the contents of his pockets.[5] So what is the back story?

According to the report in the Hemel Hempstead Gazette for 7th August the Bank Holiday Gala and Fete in the Castle grounds at Berkhampstead[6] was a splendid affair. Brigade Drill by the local Volunteer Battalion, a military band, a lengthy concert, dancing and side shows drew the crowds. Local hostelries erected marquees to provide food and much liquid refreshment. Mr. Loines, the landlord of the Castle Inn hired extra waiters for the day and amongst them was Robert Baldry. The work was non-stop and not until the "beautiful and brilliant" firework display had rounded off the evening were the waiting staff able to draw breath. It was after 11 o'clock when Robert told William Bartlett, a fellow waiter, that he was going to stay the night in the tent and Bartlett said he would stay with him. Lying down on the bruised and trampled grass they both fell asleep.

At the inquest next day Mary Loines, of the Castle Inn, stated:

I saw the deceased lying on the grass at midnight and I asked 'What are you doing here?' He did not answer but got up and walked about the tent for about five minutes. Then he said 'I am doing my duty and looking after the tent' After that I heard him

---

[4] Hemel Hempstead Gazette and West Herts Advertiser. Saturday 12th August 1882. www.britishnewspaperarchive.co.uk Accessed July 2016
[5] See copy at the end of the chapter.
[6] During most of the 19th century, and into the 20th century, there was no universally agreed way of spelling Berkhamsted - or Berkhampstead . I have used the more common 19th century version throughout

say to my husband 'Give me my bag'. My husband did so. He left the tent and I did not see him again. He did not say where he was going to.

I suspect that Robert had drunk more alcohol than he should and that he was very tired. Life can look somewhat grey in the small hours so perhaps he was comparing his present employment with the better positions he had had before. Whatever his mood he did not turn left out of the Castle grounds to start his walk home. Note that he had not collected his wages. For some reason he walked down to the railway line and an hour or two later his crushed head and mangled body were found on the "four foot way of the up-slow line."

An article in the Bucks Herald for November 1882 added a certain notoriety to the story. It reported that a memorial – a petition - signed "by the Rector and clergy of all denominations, the local magistrates, and many of the most influential inhabitants" of Berkhampstead was to be put to the Earl of Brownlow, who leased the Castle grounds and gave grants for their use, to prohibit in future the sale of intoxicating drinks in the grounds. Why? Because
The intemperance of the last Bank Holiday celebrated in the grounds, culminating in the sad death of a waiter, who staggered on to the railway and was killed, offended the moral sense of the neighbourhood.

It is not everyone who can have such an effect on the pleasure of a whole town. And might it be that the opprobrium and gossip about the accident reflected on poor Rosetta.

Who broke the news to her? Robert's older brother, John, a costermonger in Rickmansworth, was apparently summoned to identify the body. Perhaps there was a kindness shown there. The body was not a fit sight for a widow and perhaps it was suggested by the police that someone else should do that unenviable task. It must have been a terrible blow for his wife! Quite apart from her emotional loss there was the practical situation to consider. With a son of twelve, four daughters aged nine, eight, six and two and an invalid mother to care for, how could Rosetta manage? She is listed in the census as a dressmaker but how much money did that bring in? There was never a murmur of the workhouse, but life could not have been easy. Perhaps she had wealthy customers, or, more likely did piece work at home. Either way she must have worked extremely hard to feed and clothe the family. I have no certain knowledge of that period in their lives but a story in the Bucks Herald dated 16th January 1886 may indicate the difficulty of bringing up the family alone – especially a boy who would have missed his father.

Dishonest Boys: Robert Baldry aged fourteen and Goodwin Howard were charged with stealing a purse and contents, namely two watch keys, one sovereign and ten shillings, the property of Edwin Nicholls of Hemel Hempstead. Baldry was sentenced to be whipped with six strokes of the birch and Howard to twenty-one days of hard labour[7].

I can't prove that it was our Robert but he is the only Robert Baldry recorded in the 1881 census of Hemel Hempstead aged ten[8]. Robert – according to my grandmother - joined the Royal Marines as a boy. At that time boys could join at fifteen - providing they were 5 feet in height and had a thirty inch chest. Perhaps his mother thought he was getting into bad company and that she as a widow could not cope. So one mouth less to feed. By 1887 Alice had entered service, followed by Annie Maria which would have eased the household finances.

---

[7] Herts Mercury & Reformer www.britishnewspaperarchive.co.uk/ Accessed July2016

[8] As is Goodwin Howard who was 17 in the same census and was now 22 years old – which would account for the difference in sentence.

What had Robert been like as a father? We have a album of family photographs and, what is more, they were carefully labelled by my mother before she died. I suspect that this photo of Robert was taken when he was a butler. He is dignified looking man with a broad forehead, appraising eyes and mutton chop whiskers framing his chin. He looks as though he took pride in his position. Perhaps he inclined his head graciously; spoke in a grave voice from which he had endeavoured to eliminate all vestiges of broad Norfolk and the accent of rural Hertfordshire: almost the epitome of the perfect butler. And there is a hint of a smile. He could have been a warm understanding father but since his duties must have taken up almost all his time, he probably wasn't at home much. Once the family was back at Piccotts End perhaps he was less dignified, even less caring. Four months before he died he was fined 2/6d for failing to get his son regularly to school[9]. Whatever he was like as a man and a father he departed from the scene at the young age of thirty-eight, and Rosetta was left as a single mother.

What was her background? Her father, Paul Byrne, had been a hairdresser. Gran Hope kept his business card which proudly lists all his accomplishments. It says he had been apprenticed at Barteleto's in Regent Street – with all the cachet that a London hairdresser gave. He had married Mary Anne Channing in London in 1835 but by 1847 they had moved to Hemel Hempstead and there Rosetta was born. Haircutting,

---

[9] Hemel Hempstead Gazette & West Herts Advertiser 13 May 1882 www.britishnewspaperarchive.co.uk Accessed July 2016

dressing, perfuming must have been quite profitable for in 1861 Rosetta was still "a scholar" at fourteen and had not been sent into domestic service. Paul and Mary Anne may have had aspirations in that they had carte de visites[10] taken of themselves and also had a silhouette made of the young Rosetta to hang on the wall.

Sadly Paul also died young, at the age of forty-seven "within two weeks of contracting scarlet fever", according to my grandmother. Rosetta was fourteen and her only sibling, Benjamin, was eleven. Her mother kept on the shop as a "Toy and fancy article business" and was still in trade ten years later. Perhaps Rosetta was apprenticed to a dressmaker after her father's death.

Between Robert's death in 1882 and the 1891 census there was much change in the Baldry household. Old Mrs. Byrne died a year after her son-in-law. By 1891 Alice Rosetta, the eldest daughter, was a housemaid in London. Daisy, the baby of the family was still at school and Florence, at fourteen, had become a nursemaid.

And what of Annie Maria, my Gran Hope? At sixteen years old – and perhaps for a couple of years – she had been employed as a housemaid in Hemel Hempstead. Her employers were two elderly sisters, Anne and Mary Hamilton, who, according to the census were "Living on own means". She was second housemaid and there was a cook, an older housemaid and a coachman cum groom. By 1901 she was a "general domestic" at Lavant in Sussex and perhaps the only living-in

---

[10] A type of small photograph which was patented in Paris, France by photographer André Adolphe Eugène Disdéri in 1854, and became very popular.

servant to two ladies, Miss Florence Francis and her companion Miss Harriet Hopkins. She said she liked to move around. My mother said:

> At one household my mum told me that the servants after a party used to drain the dregs of the glasses into a jug and share it out. In another of her situations the butler accidentally mixed wine with the brandy and the staff took the decanter into the cellar and drank it themselves..... Not like my mild little Mum.

She does look mild – mild, conscientious, serious and with, I think, a strong likeness to her father.

How did that 'mild little Mum' become a mother? Sometime between 1901 and 1904, and working in St Albans, Annie Maria met an ex-soldier on a blind date. Benjamin Hope was "5 ft.7½ inches, brown hair and a fresh complexion" according to the crumpled and faded army records which my grandmother kept all her life. He was born in St Albans to Samuel and Louisa Hope. His mother was apparently known as the 'Mother of Sopwell Lane' and helped with all the local births and deaths. Benjamin joined the 2nd battalion of the Bedford Regiment at the age of eighteen. Since he had previously been assisting his father, who was a sweep in St Albans, the army probably seemed more attractive. In April 1897, perhaps bored by the inactivity of the barracks, he got into trouble. He was convicted of assault on a police constable and was sentenced to one month's hard labour. Not deterred by this, only six weeks after being released he was convicted of a 'felony' at Stafford Court[11] and sentenced to twenty-one days in prison with hard labour. Not a good start to an army career.

Later that year he was posted to the 1st Battalion in India, then to South Africa and the Boer War, left active service after seven years and was a reservist for five more. He returned home to St Albans and became a general labourer. He would have trained once a month to 'keep his eye in', so that a minimum of training was required to get him back to 'battle fitness' again if required. My mother asserted that he was a crack shot who represented his regiment and won prizes at the shooting range at Bisley. This is borne out because the 1st battalion in India was a shooting unit[12] and entered many competitions despite being abroad. Any soldier representing his unit was awarded a badge as shooting 'colours' for representing the unit in competition. And Benjamin had such a badge. I have been told that this meant he was obviously a marksman of some note to have achieved this accolade[13].

How long the courtship lasted I do not know, but Annie and Benjamin were married in 1905. The wedding was at St Peter's church in St Albans and their mothers – both widows – signed the register.

---

[11] The regiment was sometimes based at the Whittington Barracks, near Lichfield, Staffordshire.

[12] Soldiers who were accomplished shots or sportsmen were often grouped into one battalion to be available for practice and competition.

[12] Soldiers who were accomplished shots or sportsmen were often grouped into one

[13] Information from Steve Fuller. www.bedfordregiment.org.uk Accessed 2013

I like to think this picture was taken on his wedding day. We have no official wedding photo of the two of them together. I expect that at one time the photograph was cut out to fit into a little oval frame. Maybe Annie Maria had it on her dressing table.

The couple rented a house in Fleetville, a suburb of St Albans. A new factory had been built there in the very first years of the twentieth century by Smith's Printing Works, a firm that had moved from Fleet Street in London in order to expand its business. The firm also built a terrace of shops and several streets for their artisan workers. Arthur Road, where the Hopes lived, was one of these. I have no proof but Benjamin was most probably employed by Smith's, for it was a large company. The street was straight and lined with two identical terraces of small flat fronted houses. It is still there.

The windows had white stone surrounds which stood out from the hard red brick. The plain front doors with polished knockers opened straight onto the pavement, their steps, honed and bleached, gleamed like two rows of well-spaced teeth all down the street. Inside the house there was a tiny hall, just the width of the door. The front parlour was dark. It had an open fire with a cupboard to one side, a shelf to display china, room for chairs and a hard, shiny black sofa stuffed with horsehair. The living room behind was made cosy by a kitchen range, its oven and fender in polished steel. There was a cupboard on one side of the range. A small table stood beneath the single sash window which looked out to the garden. Beyond the living room was the scullery which had a copper and a deep sink The stairs, which were on one side of the parlour, were boxed in by a latched door and shiny brown close-boards, the colour of newly fallen conkers. There were three bedrooms. One, just big enough for a small cast iron and brass double bedstead, also had a dressing table, and a small wardrobe. The children's rooms each contained a cupboard, single bed and a few shelves with a chair on which to place clothes at night. No bathroom, of course, but the main bedroom had a stand containing a pretty china ewer and basin decorated with pink and green flowers. The lavatory and large coal shed were outside facing up the garden. In between the houses were dark arched passages leading to the back door and the garden which was long and narrow and had a brick path, edged with glazed rope-top tiles and over them spilled polyanthus, pinks and double daisies. The rent was 10/- a week.

Those details were mainly memories of my mother. My own recollections of that little house are fragmentary. Elusive smells: furniture polish, the slight mustiness of the boxed in staircase. Blurred images: the roughness of the rag rug in front of the fire: the green plush table covering that had bobbles round the edge just asking to be grabbed by little hands; the chill damp of the wooden lavatory seat outside. And do I remember the loose pages of Old Moore's Almanac threaded on rough string beside the lavatory? I could not have recognised it as the Almanac then, but I remember my mother carefully tearing off the pages for me. I only visited Arthur Road until the beginning of the Second World War when I was not yet four, but I was taken there quite often.

There, in number 22, Annie Maria and Benjamin set out to make family life. Within two years of marriage a son, Robert Benjamin was born. He was always known as Ben but nonetheless there was a nod of respect towards Annie Maria's father. There is just one photograph of the chubby, cheerful child seated on a decorative chair, his pinafore rucked around his neck and with a lace petticoat fringing his dress, taken when he was about two years old.

Three years later came Florence Daisy, my mother, born on the 13th February 1910. It was an easy birth, reported my mother, remembering that Annie had said: "I went up the road to get the evening paper and six hours later you were born." There were no more children. Was that deliberate? I don't believe they "took precautions" though my mother once told me that Gran Hope had said that after love-making her husband would say "Go on, girl, that's right. Go and have a good wee."

Both children were baptised in the galvanised iron mission church of St Paul's almost a mile away. Beyond that fact, what of them all until 1914 when life radically changed? Hardly anything.

It must have been a closed little world. Benjamin probably read a paper as he relaxed by the fire while Annie prepared tea, and headlines like the death of the suffragette Emily Davison on Derby day in June 1913 would have been exclaimed over. As the months passed unsettling incidents in Europe may have been discussed, but I daresay that most of the conversational exchanges concerned local people, affairs and gossip. It is hard for us to imagine the silence and lack of information: no television, no radio, no telephone. Pathé news had only been in cinemas for about ten years. If it was shown in the Alpha Picture Palace in St Albans were they adventurous enough to go? There was a workmen's institute built by Smith's at the end of Arthur Road which had a coffee bar, reading rooms, gymnasium and a library so if Benjamin worked for the company there were leisure time occupations there. But there was a ban on alcohol and he enjoyed a drink and chat with his mates in a pub. He may have indulged a little too much or too often, for I remember that Gran was always a little prejudiced about alcohol and touched not a drop herself – except for a little ginger wine at Christmas. Her recreation was to go to night school, presumably leaving Ben to mind the children. World affairs had to take care of themselves.

We know, however, that such affairs never do and in June 1914 with the assassination of Archduke Ferdinand in Sarajevo the simmering pot spat, bubbled and boiled over catastrophically when Britain declared war on Germany on 4th August of that year. The Recruiting Office in St Peter's Street in St Albans opened on the 11th August 1914 but by the end of that first month fewer than 100 men had enlisted out of a population of around 5,000 potentially eligible for military service.

What did Benjamin Hope do? He was one of the hundred, re-enlisting on the 14th August. He was not young, having had his thirty-seventh birthday in April, but men who had been in the army could enlist as long as they were under forty-five. He was no longer a reservist who would automatically be called up. My mother told me that he had said nobly to his wife "I am going for you, my dear, for you and the children." Did he really think that? Or did he just feel that the army life would be more exciting than shifting bricks and digging roads? Perhaps I am being unfair. After all, even Wilfred Owen could write at the very beginning of the war, "There is a fine heroic feeling about being in France and I am in perfect spirits,"[14] and at home there was a rush of emotional patriotism. Was Annie horrified or was she too swayed by that fervour? Benjamin must have travelled by train to Bedford to enlist for he was part of the 7th Bedford (Service) battalion. The battalion did not go to France until July 1915. His son, Ben, once told me that his Dad said he had done some bare-fist fighting on Salisbury Plain when they were waiting to go to France – something that he did not tell his wife or daughter. The regiment sailed from Folkestone to Boulogne

---

[14] In a letter to his mother.

and was engaged heavily on the Western front for the whole of the war.

Sadly Benjamin left no personal memories of the war. What I do have is a vivid personal memory of my mother's. Indeed, it is here that she, Florence Daisy Hope, comes into the story on her own account. It must have been a remembrance hard-wired into her memory for, as something of a closet writer, she noted it down several times, as I discovered in her papers after her death, yet it differed very little in any of them. She wrote:

> When the First World War was declared I was four years old so I don't remember my father leaving home to re-join the army. One day when I was six or seven years old, my brother Ben and I had friends in to play while Mother was out at the Adult school. We were playing zoos. Ben and his friend were under the table being lions and René and I were running around them. Suddenly there was a knock at the door and a very dirty soldier came in. We were frightened because we did not recognise my father, not having seen him for about three years. René whispered, "Shall I fetch my Dad?" and shot out of the door. Soon Pop and Mrs. Payne came round "Oh, Ben!" said Mrs. Payne, "What have they done to you?" And Dad told her why he was on leave. There had been a German sniper who was successfully shooting our soldiers in the trenches. "My officer said, 'See if you can get him, Hope' and I said, 'Well, I'd like a week's leave if I get him,' so here I am. I haven't had my boots off for a week." Mrs. Payne fetched a bowl of soapy water so that Dad could soak his feet.

The week passed quickly and Ben returned to the front, no doubt leaving the other members of the family unsettled and bereft.

Was it before he came home for that short leave or after it that this photograph was taken? I think that Ben looks about ten years old which would make Florrie about seven. I am sure neither of them was as gormless as they look. There they are in front of a painted military backdrop. Did Benjamin get the photo and keep it in his wallet?

Annie Maria left few oral memories of those war years which must have been difficult times for her. My mother told me that she was a good manager and needed to be for she had to make shift on the army pay of a shilling a day – perhaps a little more if Benjamin's marksman's qualification was recognised. She had a friend, the wife of a chemist, and used to work for her both in the house and shop. She preferred to do that than take in washing. And it must have been lonely too, and worrying. One Christmas, probably after the battle of the Somme, she put all the presents in a big clothes basket instead of in stockings. "I was just too downhearted to fill them," she told Florrie later.

The children were not affected much by wartime conditions though Florrie remembered queuing for ½lb margarine which was the week's ration for one person. Annie had put her in the queue further up the line. A policeman said to her "Where is your mother?" "Down there", Florrie replied. "Well, go and stand with her, then."

The Institute at the end of Arthur road was requisitioned by the military towards the end of the war and one or two soldiers were billeted in the houses, according to the bedrooms available. Their rank and number was chalked on the wall by each front door. Households were paid three shillings a day to accommodate one. This included payment for cooking three meals a day from the soldier's ration, which was delivered by the ration fatigue in a wheelbarrow piled with fresh meat, bread, potatoes, sugar, tea, cheese and tins of jam. Florrie moved from her little room over the alley way and shared the double bed with her mother so that Hodge Uphill, the Major's driver, a gentle young man of nineteen, could have her room. Florrie said:

> He was always whittling pieces of wood to make small toys. He would sharpen my pencils, making a beautiful point and shave off the wood with great care. And he would tease, creeping up to the window and knocking on the glass saying, 'Put that light out!' He stayed long enough for his parents and younger brother to come up from Wiltshire and visit him for a weekend. The two families became friendly but in the aftermath of war the contacts were lost and they did not keep in touch.

That could be the whole story: a fleeting memory of a young man sharpening pencils, but one afternoon in 1954 my mother and grandmother were watching television. Jeanne Heal was interviewing a man who had made pieces of miniature furniture for Queen Mary's Dolls' House at Windsor. She referred to him as 'Mr. Uphill'. 'That must be Hodge,' said my mother, and she wrote to him through the BBC. He replied saying that he would be delighted to see them again and the following spring our family went to Wilton near Salisbury where he had his shop. By then he was fifty-six years old, a tall man with a gentle smile, delicate features, and wavy hair. It was my grandmother's 80th birthday and he gave her a miniature chest of drawers. My parents kept up the friendship with the Uphills until Hodge died in the late sixties with Dulcie following him but ten months later. It was a deep and lasting friendship which arose from that wartime meeting.

Florrie had other memories of the war years:

> Other soldiers billeted in the road were not as well behaved as Hodge. One called "Titch" was always getting into trouble and was put on charge. He had to do pack drill marching up and down the road in full kit, carrying his pack and rifle. We used to follow him in a cat calling crowd, skipping or marching in step behind him, our arms swinging vigorously.

Inevitably the war had an impact on the games of the children in Arthur Road in the First World War. Ben and other boys made a dug-out in the field nearby. It was large with earth shelves for seats round the edge. Said my mother:

> We children used to light a fire in the middle and cook potatoes if we could scrounge some. We used French words like "oui, oui" and "parlez vous" and of course we sang a lot of songs like 'Take me back to dear old Blighty,' 'It's a long way to Tipperary' and 'Rose of Picardy'. There was anti-German feeling, too, among the boys. One Christmas during the war I was given a doll. Ben examined it and seeing the maker's mark on the back of its china head, said disgustedly, "That's a German doll," and without ado he broke its legs.

My mother always said that her father died from the effects of gas. The Germans first used gas at the Battle of Loos in April, 1915 – before Ben's regiment went to France. By the end of 1915 most soldiers had a smoke helmet – better known as the 'goggle-eyed booger with the tit' which was a grey flannel bag impregnated with chemicals, with two eye pieces and a rubber mouth piece. By 1917 these were replaced by a helmet made of thicker material, a one way valve at the mouthpiece and two glass eyepieces.

Benjamin was transferred to the Labour Corps sometime in 1917 because he was no longer fit for front line service, either through injury or illness. Being gassed was a classic reason for being transferred. The Labour corps carried out basic labouring tasks, moving stores, clerical and administrative duties and guard duties. In France & Belgium the men worked unarmed within the range of German guns. They often worked for weeks or even months at a time in the most dangerous conditions with only one day's rest in every seven. No soft option for an older man.

War ended in November 1918 and Benjamin came home in 1919 with three medals and a weak chest. Did he work again? I suspect not, nor can I imagine how my grandmother felt to have a husband with whom she had only spent ten years of normal married life to have a tired man with a constant cough. He must have been a resilient fellow though because my mother had no feeling that he was mentally damaged. Indeed, she, then aged nine, remembered him as:

> ...a kindly man. I remember sitting by the fire bathing the dog's paw and bandaging it up and my dad saying gently with a smile 'He will lick it better himself, child'. When I ran in to the house one day complaining that one of the children in the street had hit me he said 'You must fight your own battles. I'm not falling out with my neighbours over children's squabbles.' At the only Christmas I remember being with him, he cooked the dinner and looked after Ben and me for my Grandma Baldry was dying in London and he said to my mother: "You go, my girl. I can manage here."

In August 1920 Benjamin died in the County Tuberculosis Hospital at Ware. He was forty-three. The cause of death is given as pulmonary tuberculosis. Exacerbated by being gassed? I don't know. Nor do I know how long he was in hospital. It saddens me to think of Annie and perhaps the children toiling over to Ware from St. Albans on the train – and perhaps they could not go as often as they would have liked because of the cost.

He should have had a military funeral but there was too much demand. The Commission supplied the headstone and he was buried in the municipal cemetery in Hatfield Road, St Albans.

COMMONWEALTH WAR DEAD
GRAVE/MEMORIAL REFERENCE: E. I. 30. CEMETERY: ST. ALBANS CEMETERY.

In 1962 my grandmother was, unusually, buried in the same grave. No indication on the headstone, of course, for she was no soldier, but she too had carried the burdens of the war.

Benjamin's funeral was not paid by the Commission. Since funerals then cost about £25 I wonder how Gran paid for it. I have a memory of 'the man from the Pru' calling regularly when she was living with us and no doubt she was putting money aside for her own funeral. She was as prudent as the insurance.

But my mother should have the last word about her father who she only really knew properly for eighteen months of her life:

> He came home bearing a little rosary which he found hanging on a little wayside cross in France - all that was left of a whole village. We got to know and love him again. I remember walking with him and him laughing

because I was trying to match my stride with his. We had been to see the fireworks in the park near to the house of my Grandmother Hope. I had been frightened and he tucked me under his greatcoat. I smelt the khaki and I felt comforted. Sadly he soon became ill. He had been gassed in the war – I remember seeing that his gas mask had a split in the eye piece - and he died in 1920. I was ten years old. At his funeral I rode in a car for the first time and I hoped everyone would see me. However, all the blinds of the houses were drawn down, but René and I were able to wave to each other, she peeping round the side of the blind. I was upset at the grave side crying "Don't leave my Dad in that black hole." A kindly man, I have felt the loss of a father all my life. When I had been naughty as a child and was shut on the stairs I would wail "Oh, I want my daddy!" – although I realise now that he would probably have treated me in exactly the same way. And whenever I see in life or on television a father and daughter together it gives me a pang of sorrow, even though I have had a happy family and a mother who was a real friend.

****

Report in the Hemel Hempstead Gazette & West Herts Advertiser Saturday 12 August 1882.
On the same day an inquest was held by the coroner in the Railway Tavern, Berkhampstead, on the body of Robert Baldrey, a waiter, who resided at Piccott's End, Hemel Hempstead. Francis Rice, engine driver said he was driving the engine No.2027 from London to Tring on that morning. He started at 3.15am. As he was approaching the Berkhampstead station at 4.20 he met a train passing on the up fast line, and the driver of that engine signalled to witness that there was something in front of witness. Witness slackened his pace and looked out ahead, and he saw something lying on the four foot way of the up slow line. He stopped the engine and saw it was the deceased lying there. He got down from his engine and placed the body on the embankment, and proceeded to the Berkhampstead station and told the signalman and others of the occurrence. The stationmaster came and sent a

messenger for a doctor. When the doctor arrived witness went with him to the body of the deceased, which, by the doctor's orders, they placed on a small ladder and took it to the Railway Tavern. The body was warm when witness found it.

Inspector Penn said that on that morning about 5 o'clock he was told that a man was found dead on the railway, and he went with others to the body. Before they came to it the last witness picked up a shilling and a sixpence and gave it to the witness. Witness searched the pockets of the deceased and found a leather purse containing an old spade half guinea and an old worn shilling, three gilt shirt studs, a pawnbroker's duplicate, etc. The broken knife produced was picked up by a platelayer on the line, also a watch and a memorandum book.

Mr Robert Arne, surgeon, said he was called to the deceased, and he saw the body lying on the embankment. It was quite dead and cold. The skull was completely crushed in, and one foot severed from the leg, hanging only by a piece of skin. The injuries were sufficient to cause instantaneous death.

John Baldry, of Rickmansworth, fishmonger, identified the body as that of his brother Robert. The deceased was 38 years of age, and was a married man with five children.

Verdict: Accidental Death.

Chapter 2.

A happy childhood.

After Benjamin died Annie Maria was awarded a pension of five shillings a week for each child until they were fourteen, although, in Ben's case that was only for a year. To supplement this she briefly took in a lodger, an unhappy woman from London who arrived with her small daughter. My mother, with hindsight, said she was a drab, whining sort of young woman and added forthrightly "I think she had come to look for some man and was probably a prostitute". Once more Florrie had to move out of her little bedroom. She resented the child, and did not want to play with her or include her in the games with her friends. However, these lodgers stayed for only a few months. Life continued to be tough but my mother said she never felt deprived. Indeed, "comfort and coziness" was her summing up of her childhood.

Florrie's life was bound up with that of the other children in the road. The census of 1911 shows that there were about twenty children around the same ages as Ben and Florrie, a goodly number for play in a cul de sac where there would have been hardly any traffic. They were all children of parents who were roughly of equal status – railwaymen, jobbing gardeners, carpenters and men employed by the Smith's Printing works - with little difference in wealth or the lack of it. There was a strong boys' gang and the girls followed. They bowled hoops up and down the road, skipped, spun tops, played hopscotch on roughly chalked squares on the pavement and competed at five stones and marbles. Florrie said:

> On winter evenings we would persuade our mothers to let us out to meet under the lamp at the end of the road. It was there that we planned our campaign of Pin and

Button. A pin was pushed into a window frame with a button on a long piece of cotton. This was pulled so that the button tapped the window. Another game was Knock, Knock! Two knockers were tied with string. We would knock one door and hide. When the owner opened her door the other would knock and so on. We would hide, giggling in the shadows. But Mrs. Gillett always had a jug of water ready in the bedroom to throw over us. And it was soon "Ben! Florrie! Come along in." The one evening our mothers attended the Adult school for their weekly class, we children collected in one of the houses to play games.

In the holidays food and drink were piled into an old white wicker baby's pram and all the children went off for the day to the Nine Fields These fields figured a lot in their young lives being about 1½ miles from Arthur Road, and, naturally, their favourite place was in the far corner away from any adult intervention. The fields were those they ran over when they saw a balloon floating over dropping sand. They thought it was landing and ran far enough to miss afternoon school. There, too, they played party games and held Pin concerts and plays – admission a card of pins.
Florrie continues:

Safety pin seats were in the trees and these were usually taken by the boys who made fun and fooled about while the girls performed. Once, I remember, the boys ran off with the pins. This ended in a fight. At one concert René – who was called Tilly in those days was the star turn. Arrayed with a gilded sun made of cardboard over her head, she started her monologue: "I am the Sun" but another girl shouted furiously "Oh get off, Tilly, it's not your turn yet". René, furious at being denied her party-piece, leapt down and a scuffle ensued.

One little girl, Rosebud Smith, always went home to fetch her dinner, coming back with meat and salad on a plate. This was because she liked vinegar and sugar on her lettuce. It was she who used to play dolls with me. Once we cut off a doll's hair and then rubbed camphorated oil on its head hoping the hair would grow.

One Saturday morning, Tilly and I should have appeared in a play, but having had a tempting offer of a ride in a horse and cart to Sandridge about four miles away – a great treat – we forsook our friends and went. We sat up with the carter, admiring the glossy back and bright harness of the horse and enjoyed the unfamiliar high-up view of the countryside. Unfortunately our way went by the field which was thronged with our friends and we were jeered at by all the company.

"Take me fishing with you," Florrie would coax her brother as he gathered up his fishing gear. He rarely agreed but occasionally she was allowed to follow several paces behind him and his friends as long as she carried the worms in a pail.

I think of my mother's childhood as being very sociable – learning to give and take in a friendly gang of peers that knew one another well. And though they had little money they used their imagination and made their own fun. The freedom of the Arthur Road children would be much envied by children in the twenty-first century. As a child I used to set off with my cousins across the fields and make fires in a dell, which was the remains of an old chalk pit, or go into Hatfield Park a mile from home, pick daffodils, ride imaginary horses through the woods and in winter toboggan there till frozen, so not much change one generation later.

What of our own children in the 1970s? Living in London suburbia gave no scope for wandering in fields and wood, though Nell with her friends almost set fire to an oak tree on the pavement in the next road and Kate and a friend would cycle the streets for two or three hours before they were eleven. As they grew older they walked the dog in nearby parks but they lacked the opportunity to disappear for the whole day without parental concern.

It is reported that children's "roaming range" in 1915 was six miles. In 2015 it is said to be 300 yards.[15]

Present concerns are that children will be molested, plucked from the street by a paedophile or confronted by inadequate men flashing all? My mother and her friend René acted robustly in the latter situation:

> We were walking along the lane near the railway in the rain one day and a man passed on his bicycle. We thought nothing of that but then he turned round and passed us again, smiling in a silly sort of way. When he returned for the third time we saw that his penis lay along the crossbar of his bicycle. We threw our umbrellas at him and ran off. Of course, we didn't tell our mothers.

She told me this story lightheartedly so that I was not unduly afraid when a similar thing happened to me in my teens. I got into an old fashioned railway carriage with no corridor and began to read. Other passengers got out until there was only one man sitting opposite. When I looked up from my book I saw he was wearing a fatuous smile and unbuttoned trousers. I looked blank, did not meet his eyes, resumed reading and got out at the next station.

Indoor play for my mother was simple. "Always dolls. Making clothes for them, pretending they were ill and needed nursing". She also liked to paint and draw, as did her brother. Indeed she remembered that when her father was alive he

---

[15] www.wildlifetrusts.org/everychildwild Accessed 2015

stopped her from pestering Ben when he was engaged with paper and pencil. And there were household chores to be done. Florrie had to clean the silver on a Saturday morning and Ben cleaned shoes. Sweets were bought for them – a ½ d or 1d worth – but they had no set pocket money. And, of course, she added, "I did have books to read".

Besides Dollytown, my mother kept two more of her early books. They are well-worn, their torn covers clumsily stitched on with brown thread. One has the snappy title: *The History of Little Bo-Peep the Shepherdess: shewing how she lost her sheep and couldn't tell where to find them*. It has crude coloured pictures and the story pulls no punches. Bo-Peep is told that she should be locked up and be given only bread and water for a month because she failed to do her job properly. She falls into the hands of a wicked old woman and her ugly son who tie her to a tree and beat her. Aided by fairies, all is well in the end and her sheep agree not to wander again. The other is Aunt Louisa's London Toy Book, called *The Robin's Christmas Eve*. The illustrations are richly coloured but it is a sickly tale about a starving robin who finds shelter in an English church. I realise that they were first published in the 1860s so my mother must have had them second-hand.

Taking them from my mother's bookshelf I saw that inside the front cover of each there is the name Edith T. Ure written faintly in pencil in an adult hand. I had never noticed this before and the surname triggered a dim memory. I was given a dolls' china tea set by an old lady when my mother and I visited her house. I have a shadowy remembrance of the occasion but it is too vague to recall. Later my mother told me: "Miss Ure gave you the tea set because you had just had your fourth birthday and she had received it as a present when she, too, was four years old."

The tea set is charming and complete. The pale aquamarine transfer decoration depicts early paddle steamers and a harbour garlanded with flowers. There are six cups and saucers, an elegantly shaped teapot, milk jug, slop bowl, a comparatively large sugar bowl and two tiny tin teaspoons. It now sits unused in our china cabinet but I enjoyed it most when our small daughters dressed their china dolls, Sabu and Lucy, in their best clothes on a rainy day and a solemn tea party was held with polite Cranford-like conversation[16].

I had never connected the tea set with my mother's books and do not remember my mother saying how she had acquired them. So who was Miss Ure? It is easier nowadays with genealogy websites to satisfy one's curiosity.

I know now that she was Edith Torrington Ure born in Boxgrove in Sussex in 1852 where her father was a headmaster. He died young and in 1881 her mother, Edith and Alice, her older sister moved to St Albans. They lived in George Street near the Abbey and earned enough as governesses to keep one servant. Edith remained a spinster and died in St Albans in 1941, a year or so after she gave me the tea set. But when did she give my mother the books?

George Street is more than a mile away from Fleetville, so they were not near neighbours. It is only supposition, but could my grandmother have been employed by her before she was married? If so, the association between them could have lasted from when Florrie was a child to when she took me to see Miss Ure in 1939. It would be typical of my grandmother to keep up the connection if she felt that Miss Ure was lonely in old age.

The little family of the three Hopes was augmented from time to time by relatives. Old Mrs. Baldry died in 1920 but it is likely that she stayed with her daughters in turn, not an unusual arrangement. She was with the Hopes on the night of the 1911 Census and with Annie's sister, Alice and her husband, when

---

[16] Elizabeth Gaskell: *Cranford*. A novel of village life. Published 1853

she died in 1920, having been visited by Annie Maria at Christmas, 1919.

Then there was Florrie, Annie's next sister. Her husband, Harry (Tug) Wilson was a deep sea diver and absent for long periods, working as far away as Hong Kong. Her niece and nephew called Florrie the Flying Aunt because she would arrive suddenly and unexpectedly and depart in the same way, bringing her belongings in a large wicker laundry basket which still serves as our dressing up box. Florrie had no children and I suspect the marriage was somewhat tempestuous. She worked as a high-class cook when Harry was away but at one time they separated and she stayed with the Hopes. Then they came together again and she looked after him in his last illness. Harry Wilson had a gurgling laugh and his waistcoat buttons strained across a beer belly. He once gave me a necklace of striped red glass beads saying they came from Red Indians. I'm not sure if this was true but being interested in the Wild West – and always on the side of the Indians - I cherished them. Aunt Florrie was not comfortable and calm like my grandmother. She was spiky and lively as a ferret.

Relations who became a more permanent part of lives of the Hopes were the Hangarters who came to live in St Albans in 1920. Annie Maria's sister, Alice, had married James Hangarter, a German who she had met when they were both in service in London. His story, like that of Hodge's, is unusual and has become a part of family folklore. Born in 1873 in a little village at the lower part of Lake Constance, Germany, he moved into Switzerland to find work in a hotel and soon afterwards came to England. In 1901 he was a waiter at St John's College, Battersea and ten years later he applied for and was granted British citizenship. In 1913, their only child, Marie Rosetta was born and James had been promoted to butler at the College. In the first half of 1914 his niece, Florence Hope aged four, visited Battersea with her mother:

It was before the war and I remember a basement kitchen and trains, I think, going past because we could see them from the high windows and I was given a glass of milk and a very hard plain biscuit.

Although James was forty-four in the summer of 1918 he was called up and was placed in the Labour Corps and then transferred to the Reserve in April 1919.

My mother recalled that the family lived with them for a while at 22 Arthur Road until they were able to rent a house further down the road on the opposite side. She also said that for a while they stopped calling themselves Hangarter and went by the name of James. I don't know when they decided to do this. Perhaps it was even after the war when the loathing of everything German became more intense. This hatred redounded upon them for when James was demobbed and applied for his old job at the College his application was unsuccessful even though he had been employed there for twenty years and had fought on the British side. Still, with the help of the Bursar, who had valued his services, he secured a post as Head Porter at Oaklands College between St Albans and Hatfield after they had moved from London. Oaklands had been bought for use as an Agricultural College for Hertfordshire in 1920. It was not perhaps such a prestigious post as he had held at Battersea but he must have been appreciated for when he died in 1965, aged ninety-two, the Principal of the college went to the funeral. Alice had died fifteen years earlier at the age of seventy-seven.

My mother was fond of Uncle James and remembered small details of his life and habits.

When cutting meat he always sharpened the knife before – but only once, one stroke and that was it! After a meal he always filled a tall jug with boiling water and placed the dirty cutlery in it – making the cutlery much easier to clean.

As a child on the few occasions we visited their house I did not warm to Alice Hangarter and my mother said forthrightly "She was a strait-laced old stick. I never liked her." Uncle James was jolly, warm and friendly. He looked very German, wore a smart dark pin-striped suit with a waistcoat adorned with a watch and chain. He was cheerful and had a fine chuckle. Their daughter, Marie, two years younger than Florrie, was a playmate and friend.

School did not feature much in my mother's memories. Both she and Ben went to the junior school in Fleetville, the most modern elementary school in St Albans, built in 1909. It was large, having 300 juniors and 120 infants. It must have been daunting for five year olds starting school in those days. No play groups or nursery schools to help them to settle in and perhaps little thought given to their bewilderment. Still, I suppose that the close children's community of Arthur Road meant that there were older girls who would take the younger ones under their wings. Florrie said she did not shine at school – other than as teacher's pet. I imagine her neatly attired in her smocked pinafore, her chestnut hair secured by ribbon with a large bow, bustling about filling the inkwells, making sure that her teacher's pencils were sharp and that there were new sticks of chalk on the shelf of the blackboard.

Florrie enjoyed games, needlework, drawing and painting, music and singing but in a time when spelling and grammar really mattered, her spelling let her down.– "I only learned to spell when I began to do crosswords and play Scrabble after we retired," she said, so writing was a burden. However, I think she did better than she thought. She read the parts of Pyramus and Lysander in A Midsummer Night's Dream and her copy is carefully underlined with extra directions: "Lies down and

SNORES"[17]. She had a genuine love of poetry, inspired by an English teacher, Miss Grinling, who she remembered fondly. Much verse was learned by heart and when higher up the school she was chosen to recite Tennyson's *The Lady of Shallot* at the school concert. She told me:

> I was really quite confident. I had been taught well and I stood up on the stage and recited it dramatically – all nineteen verses. But I let myself down at the end because I finished triumphantly:
> But Lancelot mused a little space
> He said, "She has a lovely face;
> God in his mercy lend her grace
> The **Sh**ady of **L**allot."

Her poetry textbook contains many of the same long poems that I studied at school with equal pleasure: *The Ancient Mariner, The Deserted Village*. Her love of poetry was reciprocated by an elderly neighbour who lived next door. Mr. Hiskett was a keen gardener and spent much time in his shed that had a large window to let in the sunlight to encourage his seeds and cuttings. I don't know how he discovered that the girl at number 22 enjoyed poetry but it happened and she used to go into his garden, sit on the work bench, her black stockinged legs swinging and she would read Longfellow and Tennyson to him as he pottered about with his plants. Longfellow's Hiawatha was a favourite and she could still quote long sections of it well into old age. It was a pleasant pastime which was eventually halted by Mrs. Hiskett who spoke to Florrie's mother and meetings were stopped. Florrie realised much later that Mrs. Hiskett thought something else was going on in the garden shed. "But it was completely innocent."

---

[17] Her copy was a Plain-Text Shakespeare published by Blackie. A note at the front assures teachers that "The text omits everything undesirable in class reading". Nothing salacious to giggle over.

Florrie was not only good at poetry and filling inkwells. She was an efficient captain of the netball team and continued to play for several years after she left school. She also shone at needlework and the patterns she had to make for baby's nightdresses and pants are meticulous and neat, the writing and measurements carefully drawn. She must have been proud of them for she kept them all her life. Her granddaughter, Nell, also paid attention to detail when she was interested in a subject. She mostly used school as a social club but when it came to cookery classes she prepared her ingredients carefully the night before, covered her basket with a clean tea towel and at school wrote down her recipes with exemplary tidiness.

Sunday school featured in Florrie's life though I am not sure that it contributed much to her religious education. She told me that one teacher wore a straw round brimmed hat which caused hilarity. One of the boys would sit next to her and the others would pass tiny balls of silver paper by sleight of hand. He would try to put these into the brim of the hat and the children had the pleasure of seeing them roll round as the teacher bent and nodded her head. Otherwise the lessons were probably much the same as those in my own day: sitting in groups in a cold church hall, sticking stamps with bible pictures on them in our attendance cards and just occasionally having a religious story told vividly and well. I was never keen to go and had to be persuaded.

I didn't even have outings as an incentive. In Florrie's time Sunday school outings were still Red Letter days on the calendar. The Fleetville children went by charabanc to Bricket Wood near Watford and there, with London Sunday Schools who came by excursion trains, they enjoyed the Bricket Wood Fairgrounds which faced each other across the green. One of them, known as Gray's Fair would provide a "children's tea of Bread and Butter, Watercress, Currant, Seed Cake and Good tea for 6d".[18] Did they squash the watercress into the bread and butter to make a sandwich?

Life was not all school or even play in the street. Mrs. Payne and Mrs. Hope took their two girls to Margate to enjoy a few days at the sea. And I was also surprised to find among my mother's papers a small autograph book. On its pastel coloured pages was a mixture of familiar aphorisms written by members of the family and verses written in by friends up to 1927. She persuaded Robert Baldry, her uncle in the marines, to fill a page. Whether this was written when the Hopes visited him in Plymouth or when he came to St Albans I do not know. His contribution was short

> A bird may sing with a broken wing
> But not with a broken
> NECK

She took the book with her when she and René travelled by train to visit the British Empire Exhibition at Wembley in September 1924. Quite brave for two fourteen year old girls who had not travelled much other than with their mothers to Margate. It was a huge spectacle that ran for two summer seasons and attracted millions of visitors. Built from scratch on a green field site, the exhibition was a showcase for goods and produce from the Empire countries. There was an amusement

---

[18] From Away for the Day: The Railway excursion in Britain 1830 to the present day Arthur and Elizabeth Jordan. Silver Link Publishing 1991.

park, a stadium for mass entertainments, and the world's first bus station. The Hongkong pavilion had a street of Chinese shops and the two girls must have gone into The China Product Co. for an assistant had written the name in the book adding the Chinese characters. There is another entry reading: "Chan Sum from Hongkong". Perhaps they were rather taken with FAZALILLAH who wrote his name and "Punjab, India" and added his native script, for his name appears on three pages.

The Church girls' club at St. Paul's was a great meeting place. My mother told me that the leader – Miss Quick:

> – even persuaded mother and Mrs.Payne to let René and I go on holiday alone when we were fifteen. We went to Hastings where Miss Quick had a friend. I remember two things about it: getting badly sunburnt; giggling so much that we wet ourselves and the dye from a red cushion stained our dresses. We were giggling because the landlady had come in when we were eating cream cakes instead of her plain ones.

Meanwhile Ben at fourteen years old had become an apprentice with Howard Grubb and Sons Ltd., astronomical instrument makers. The firm had taken over the Smith's Printing works in Fleetville – very near the end of Arthur Road. It was the beginning of his training as an engineer. He soon learned how to make his own wireless. Florrie was not always happy about this:

> He made his own sets and had amplifiers for them. The aerial went through the ceiling to my bedroom so if the noise got too loud I used to pull it out of the socket.

However, when Ben was fiddling with his radio or had friends in, Florrie and her mother would light a fire in the big bedroom, take up their supper and have a bath there.

Grubbs moved away from St Albans in 1925 and Ben had to finish his apprenticeship elsewhere. Like his mother he seems to have enjoyed changing jobs quite often for between 1925 and 1940 he moved firm six times. In each job he gained experience and training as an engineer. In 1942 he moved to de Havillands in Hatfield as a supervisor responsible for converting an empty factory and installing equipment to make Aircraft jigs and tools. Two years later he was put in charge of the Jig and Tool section which employed 300 men. There they worked on the Mosquito and Hornet aircrafts.

I daresay that, being a boisterous and sociable fellow, he soon had his own male occupations and friends and Florrie and her mother became particularly close. Annie had had few enough years with a husband and she must have valued her daughter's companionship. Some weekends, however, Florrie would stay with her best friend René whose father, Mr. Payne, known as Pop, had been put in charge of the Sewage station at Nast Hyde, near Colney Heath, a few miles from St Albans.

> My visits to Nast Hyde always started the same way: meeting my friend René and her mother in St. Albans market place at 8.00pm. Their shopping done, we would walk down London Road to the Great Northern Railway Station to catch the Hatfield train and we would get out at Nast Hyde halt. We were met by Pop Payne. It was dark and silent! Just an owl hooting. We turned right, passing

one house and after bearing right we passed a few cottages and so came to their clapboard house. Pop Payne's engine room was his pride, everywhere was shining being polished with oiled cotton waste - so different from the smell of "Iten," as Pop called it, from the sewage beds. We were soon indoors sitting by the log fire and in the lamp light, drinking our mugs of cocoa. Then to bed, armed with candles and hot bricks. The bedroom was icy cold, the wind rattling through the wooden walls. Tucked down in our feather beds we heard the last train at the halt, and the voice of the porter across the field saying "Goo'night, mind how yer go," and so to sleep.

One Sunday morning Pop called up the stairs "Look out of the window." It had been raining heavily in the night and the brook had overflowed. Fortunately Pop had raised the paths to the privy and barns with bricks and boards, for the house was on an island and the ducks were swimming away up the field[19].

Mrs. Payne did not always shop in St Albans but walked the mile or so through Roe Green to Hatfield Newtown, then an area of shops and small houses which clustered round the road leading from old town of Hatfield to St Albans. Among the shops she patronised was J. Tingey & Sons Ltd. a small grocery business with a post office. One Saturday evening in the autumn of 1924 she remarked – probably so that she could inveigle the girls into helping to carry the shopping baskets –"You ought to come shopping with me. There are two nice boys in the grocery shop in Hatfield." This suggestion turned out to be fateful for Florrie.

---

[19]Published in an article by Brian Lawrence in Hertfordshire Countryside July 2000

Chapter 3.

The Tingey Branch

If the Paynes had not moved to Colney Heath I suppose my mother and father would not have met, for he was one of the "nice boys" in the grocer's shop.

My father, Randall John Tingey, was born in 1908 and was a Hatfield boy through and through. Tingeys had lived in Hatfield since the beginning of the nineteenth century when a John Tingey and his wife Elizabeth came from Therfield, near Royston looking for work. They lived in the North Road for many years and in the 1851 census John is listed as a brick maker with four children.

Hatfield is the stage where most of this story is set so I should paint in the scenery. One day my mother came home from a jumble sale proudly carrying an old Pigot's Directory which described the town in 1851 thus:

Hatfield is a market town in the parish of Bishop's Hatfield, 19 miles NNW of London – eligibly and agreeably situated on the declivity of a hill, west of the River Lea, upon the Great North Road, and in the midst of luxuriant pasture and corn lands... Hatfield House, the seat and residence of the present Marquis of Salisbury commands the attention of the stranger on entering the town.

In the early twentieth century Hatfield was a small town of some 3½ thousand inhabitants and covered much the same area as when it was recorded in Domesday. Its survival relied on surrounding agriculture and the activity which resulted from the presence of a Royal palace in the sixteenth century – where Princess Elizabeth was confined during her sister's reign - and later the seat of the Marquis of Salisbury. It benefited from the traffic on the main coach road to the North, but it was when the Great Northern railway was laid, on its way from London to

Peterborough, that the town began to grow. Kelly's Directory for 1851 stated:
Half a mile to the west of the town, on the St Alban's Road, a great many new houses have been erected, which are called Hatfield New Town.

Inhabitants of the old town called the area "California" because it was so far west. In 1848 seven acres had been sold in a number of plots making an undistinguished settlement mainly consisting of small terraced houses on the north side of the St Albans Road, some built of the yellow London Stock bricks and others of attractive Hertfordshire flints. There were five Right of ways which divided the houses, narrow lanes which went up to Stockbreach Common behind.

Among the first buildings to have been erected were beerhouses and pubs to provide leisure time for the navvies who came to build the railway. The Gun, at the corner of Wellfield Road, the White Lion, Boar and Castle and the Robin Hood were still there when I was a child but in the early days there were many more. A number of small shops, mostly developed from dwelling houses, served the area. The south side of the road remained fields and allotments until the 1920s.

The area soon became known as "Newtown" and, seeing the opportunity for making a better living, the Tingey family moved there. Whereas Gran Hope's family had a tradition of going into "Service", the Tingeys were more independent. One son, John, who already had a baker's shop in the old town, moved his business to Newtown and kept it until his death in 1883. In 1869 his younger brother Jonathan Edmund – Randall's grandfather - took over the lease of a small grocery business close to his brother's shop. He was twenty-six years old.

A few months before he had married Arabella Grovestock, a girl who lived next door but one to his parents.

They were married in a church in Somers Town, Camden and no family members signed the register. Perhaps Arabella was in service there. However they soon returned to Hatfield because only three months later J.E., as I will now call him, agreed to pay £18 a year rent for the shop and five roomed house, plus £15 for the "Fixtures in House and Shop and utensils in trade and business" The contents of the shop included such things as: *a Mahogany top counter with thirteen drawers, 2 uprights crossbar and desk, a Coffee mill and Pepper mill, 2 Pickling Pots and dish. 2 Pair of Copper scales, 7 Brass Weights and 4 iron ditto, one 14lb, one 7lb, one 4lb and one 2lb, Patent Scale and flour ditto, A Treacle can, Vinegar cask with brass tap, 6 tea canisters, 3 tobacco jars, 3 pewter vinegar measures, a salt saw, a meat saw, 2 burners and gas fittings, 2 bacon knives.*

There were four small bedrooms above the shop and ten children were born by 1889. Arabella herself became an invalid and for a few years before her death from bronchitis in 1894 was in a wheel chair. When the only way to get her upstairs was to haul her up by ropes through a large trap door in the ceiling of the shop the family moved to a small house in one of the Right of Ways. The eldest of three boys died at the age of nine, but Edmund Thomas – always known as Tom - and John, seven years younger, grew to manhood and both went into the family firm when they were thirteen. Of the seven girls only three were to marry, two others died young. Jess, the second eldest, took on the rôle of housekeeper after her mother died. Ruth, the youngest, became a teacher in the local school and later was a secretary at Longmore's the Hertford Solicitors for many years. She remained unmarried and lived at home. The last two were personifications of Cranford type spinsters as I remember, but it is not yet my story.

Perhaps this photograph was taken shortly after Arabella's death. There they all are in front of the shop.

The business prospered for J.E. had many irons in the fire. An 1899 directory described it as "Grocers, Ironmongers, Glass and China dealers, Furniture dealers and Post Office." He also sold leather, corn, and was for a time agent for Coventry Eagle bicycles.

John remembered that, on coming home from school, he and Tom would go out with a basket of fish to sell. Most of this trade took place in a shop no bigger than the ground floor of an ordinary house, though the furniture was stored in a building nearby. Customers came not only from Hatfield but in surrounding villages and hamlets and were served by pony and trap. John often went round the town to take orders.

Here he is holding the reins. Josh, one of the assistants stands in front.

By 1901 J.E. could afford to look for a larger house. He found one a hundred yards up the road next to the Robin Hood pub. Rose Cottage was a commodious early nineteenth century house with a walled garden. J.E. had gone up in the world for his neighbours were a doctor and a timber merchant, both of whom sported two servants. By this time both sons were still at home but Maude had died, unmarried, and two daughters, Arabella and May were already wed. J.E. lived there until his death from a stroke in 1924. That was eleven years before I was born but a large photograph of him hanging in my grandparent's house made him part of the family. He stands a little pugnaciously on the door step of Rose Cottage, his beard as shaggy as his dog. Randall remembered:

52

As a child I was rather scared of him. He was a Victorian figure, tall and bearded. I remember him in the old shop sitting on a chair by a sloping Dickensian desk, chatting to customers as they came and went. He bred and showed Old English sheep dogs and won prizes with them. A shed at the end of the cobbled path of the garden of Rose Cottage was filled with cups and lines of rosettes on the wall. I stayed clear of the dogs for Grandad warned "Don't you touch that dog. It will bite you." He was public spirited, being on the Parish Council and serving as a special constable.

According to Eric, Randall's older cousin, J.E. had twinkling eyes and a good sense of humour. Fond of his whisky he would imbibe it at The Gun public house on the corner of Wellfield Road with his cronies. Randall recalled that he indulged at other times:

After a long day of trading in the pony and cart and doubtless a few settling of transactions over a drop or two in pubs, he would tie the pony's reins to the front rail of the cart and drop off to sleep, letting the pony bring him home. Ruth and Jess sometimes had to send a message to the shop so that my dad could help them to put him to bed.

Harry Ewington, one of his employees, remembered: "He was kind to animals but his pet aversion was boys. In cold weather when I was on the trap with him the rug would be whipped off my knees and put on the pony's back."[20]

---

[20] From a reminiscence written by Harry Ewington in 1957

In 1909 when he was 66 years old J.E. decided to retire.

The partnership of J.E.Tingey & Sons was dissolved and the two sons took over the business. Perhaps it was then that the boys decided to modernise and put in a new shop window which caused much talk in Newtown. And the first floor, once filled with the family, was used for storage of goods.

When I was a child there was much coming and going between the various Tingey families. There was lots of gossip, laughter, stories about customers, in-jokes, invitations to tea and large gatherings at Christmas, and undoubtedly it was the same a generation before. Eric used to visit Rose Cottage at tea time when J.E. would, more often than not, be toasting bloaters on a fork over the fire. And Ruth used to take the young Eric to St Etheldreda's church on Sunday mornings and afterwards he would be given Sunday dinner at Rose Cottage, his grandfather having scraped the homegrown horseradish to accompany the roast beef. Ruth obviously tried to look after her nephews' religious education for Randall said that after tea on Sundays they would be persuaded to sing hymns around the piano. And sometimes Ruth would take them to St Luke's church where the boys took turns to pump the organ.

Vic Cull, a friend of my father's, had a less comfortable memory of Rose Cottage. As a small boy he would deliver bread about tea time and look with envy at the rich fruit cake on the kitchen table ready for tea. "They never offered me a slice." It was a cake that the two maiden ladies valued for many years for they told my mother that they always had a slice of the Australian fruit cake for tea. "It's very nice," said Jess firmly. "And it keeps us regular."

Randall was the eldest of John's four children. He was christened with his mother's family surname. On the front pages of the family bible her father, Isaac, listed all his children's births with meticulous detail. I struggle to read them on the yellowed pages, the ink faded and the pencil entries faint. Emilie Persa, the eldest, was Randall's mother. Then followed Helena Mary, Elizabeth Francis, George Hayden, William Joseph, Edith Kate, Charles Frank and Harry. They were all born between 1881 and 1892, and only Edith Kate did not survive childhood.

Isaac Randall, himself, was born in Hatfield in 1841, but when he was eighteen he joined the 81st regiment of Foot in 1858 – a regiment known as the Loyal Lincoln Volunteers. Why a Lincolnshire regiment? Had he found work further north as a boy? He embarked for India in 1859 and amongst other campaigns fought in the Second Afghan war. He became a Colour Sergeant and carefully preserved his medal for good conduct and long service. When he married Fanny Bilton in 1880, a girl who lived two doors away from the Randall family in childhood, he was still listed as a soldier, but by the next year he was a Gate Porter at the Fore Street Lodge of Hatfield House where Emilie was born. Later he moved to the Station Lodge which stood beside the imposing wrought iron gates to the Park.[21]

---

[21] These were erected in honour of the visit from Queen Victoria in 1846

In this sadly faded picture Isaac is on the right[22]. Randall recalled:

> He was short and stocky with a white beard. I was in awe of him. He was very strict with his children. I do not remember his wife. On occasions I went to dinner at the

---

[22] There is a curious story about Isaac: Amongst my father's papers there is a creased and smudgy photocopy of a handwritten statement which reads:
> 19 April 1880
> I, Isaac Randall agree to do all the duties required as Lodge Porter at Hatfield Park at 18/-per week (paid monthly) subject to reduction of 1/- per week if I increase 14lbs in weight – or 2/- per week if I increase 28lbs in weight. And on the contrary if I reduce my weight 14lb I expect to get 19/- per week & if 28lbs 20/- per week.   One Month's notice to leave on both sides. Signed: J R Dagg [agent] I Randall
> Witness: Thomas Cain.

The archivist at Hatfield House felt that the Marquis of Salisbury, who was notoriously untidy, would not have cared a jot about the appearance of his employees. So was it a joke, though Isaac did not seem to be a man who would appreciate one? Surely the agent's signature was forged – for he was a generation older than Isaac and hardly likely to be involved. Thomas Cain was a local policeman, three years younger than Isaac and perhaps they were friends. It remains an amusing puzzle.

lodge instead of going home because mother had gone to London and on one occasion tripe was on the menu. This I could not stomach but being afraid to say so I ate it for the first and only time in my life. My uncle George was banned from entering the Park for three months as a boy. He and his friends had set fire to a tree there. For a punishment they were not allowed to go into the Park and his father insisted that George had to wait and enter the side door which as outside of the Park Gates.

I suspect that the Colour Sergeant's parade ground roar must have often dampened the liveliness of his seven children. But he was proud of them. In his Bible he recorded the appointment of his daughter Helena as a "learner" in the Post Office and wrote down all the later military achievements of his sons.

Emilie went into service and in 1901 she was employed by a shopkeeper and his wife in Islington. She is listed in the Census as the one General servant which does not sound exciting. I know nothing about her courtship with John but they were married in 1906. Randall and his brother Roland were born in Belmont Cottages in Newtown, next to the Boar and Castle pub and close to the Tingey's shop. My father remembered little of it except that the lavatory was in the garden next to the cart shed in the fourth right of way where the van horse was stabled. I suspect this picture was taken in the small garden there. For in 1913 when Randall was five, the family moved to a house called Longway in Roe Green – more than a mile from Newtown. That small village which lay south of Hatfield parish consisted of four farms, a few larger houses, cottages, one beerhouse and the Old Fiddle pub where one could also buy a few sweets at a side door. There was also a small tin chapel or Mission room in which various activities were held, such as Sunday school, Evening service, Women's Institute, private parties at Christmas time and other occasions. "It had a bell with bell rope", said Randall,

> which was used for Church services and was pulled on occasions by unauthorised persons. One of which was at around 1am during a party. A number of complaints were received because of the noise awakening sleepers far and near. The room was the scene of Sunday school plays, one of which saw me as an Eastern guard with a broomstick topped with a cut out executioner's axe. My one and only stage appearance. My mother was an active member of the newly formed W.I. and she was greatly embarrassed when we boys, with others, used to peer in at the windows. And imagine her shame when the perpetual volley of stones rattling down the tin roof was found to be the work of her sons.

Since 1951 when much of Hatfield was developed as a New Town, Roe Green has been chewed up, swallowed and regurgitated as South Hatfield with many roads of box like houses mostly named, with little imagination, after trees or birds, which gives little sense of the previous history of the area. There are roundabouts, new shops, a church and, largest of all, a campus of the University of Hertfordshire. When I was small Roe Green differed little from when the Tingeys moved there. When I was a child we often used to walk through the fields of

Holliers' farm on a Sunday afternoon. Running ahead of my parents when I was about four years old I scrambled over a stile, fell off on the other side into a patch of virulent nettles. I can recall the sore prickling as I lay in bed that hot summer evening drenched in calamine lotion. The dock leaves that my father had gathered instantly were too few to give relief. In spring my father would gather the tips of the hawthorn buds and offer them to me, calling them bread and cheese. In autumn we would snatch berries from the same trees that lined the path and chuck them at one another. And sometimes on Sunday mornings my father and I would walk to a field where mushrooms nestled in the long grass and take some home for breakfast. All these activities my father had also enjoyed as a boy.

John Tingey's brother, Tom had already moved to Roe Green having built two houses romantically called Ivanhoe and Kenilworth. Tom had a second son, Rex as well as Eric. John and Emilie's other two children, Norman and Joan were all born in Roe Green during the First World War. A clan of Tingeys was established.

Emilie's life as housewife and mother was overshadowed by the tragic events within her own family. All four of her brothers went to war in 1914. George was the luckiest for in the Army Service Corps he came through ostensibly unscathed. Charles, who had begun a career as a policeman, joined the Coldstream Guards. He lost an arm and was invalided out in 1916. He returned to the police force and eventually became Deputy Chief Constable for Hertfordshire. William, who was a Lance Corporal in the Royal Engineers, was killed by a stray bullet as he walked behind the lines in 1916. Harry, a sergeant in the Hertfordshire Regiment, died in the last year of the war having been awarded the Distinguished Conduct Medal. One of the family – and the handwriting suggests it was one of his sisters - carefully recorded the citation in the family bible, noting that it was an extract from Special Brigade orders dated 20th May 1918:

For conspicuous gallantry and devotion to duty on March 22nd 1918 and on numerous occasions during the operation. He organised counter attacks with the utmost gallantry and led his men with amazing daring. Throughout the operations he behaved with the utmost courage. He led his men with great gallantry on March 25th

Helena, having started as a Post Office learner became an assistant in Bicester and starting in 1906 she worked as a clerk in the Post office in Coventry for five years. During the war she moved to the West End of London. She was doing well. However, I have been told that her fiancée was killed and in the words of the time "she got religious mania" and used to wander in the churchyard. No doubt overwork and grief caused a nervous breakdown. She became a patient at Hill end Hospital near St Albans and was later transferred to Arlesey, a mental hospital in Bedfordshire. Sad to say she was never released and there was a silence in the family about her. Her mother visited at times, driven there by one of her sons and my parents visited in later years though they never talked about it. Helena, my father's Auntie Nell, died in 1960. Perhaps hers was the worst tragedy.

Fanny Randall, the mother of this family, was spared all the sadness and bereavement for she died in the first autumn of the war. For all those reasons Emilie could not have enjoyed much support and attention from her own kin.

Joan, born in 1916, and the youngest of Emilie and John's children, told me:

> Roly was the weak one of the family. He had convulsions as a child and Mother always cosseted him. And Randall was a nervous and slightly delicate child. His mother believed that he was never the same after he went, as a

small boy, for a visit up to London to stay with his father's sister, May. She thought the house was very dirty. He became ill and after that often had bilious attacks and headaches.

Indeed Randall remembered sitting on the old sofa in the kitchen at Longway with a warm shawl wrapped round his head. I know nothing more about his early childhood other than the story that Grandma Tingey told me. She was taking Randall and Roly out to visit a prim and critical aunt. She dressed Randall in his new mustard coloured coat with buttoned leggings. He looked so smart and she felt so proud. She had to leave him while she put Roly in his pram. When she was ready Randall was nowhere to be found. She searched the house. Out into the yard she went and there were sounds of splashing in the privy. There he was vigorously stirring the contents of the pan with a large stick, his mustard suit splattered and messy. "I wept", she said. I think this mishap must have been something of an aberration for Randall was a serious little boy and, like so many eldest children, anxious to please.

The Tingeys, like the Hopes in St Albans, had soldiers billeted with them from several regiments during the war. Indeed, they were allocated six soldiers who were crammed into two bedrooms. They were boisterous young men and Randall remembered being tossed in a blanket when he was seven years old.

> I was a little scared of this but they said I had to be initiated. One of the soldiers painted pictures, usually scenes from memory from being out on route marches. Once I endeavoured whilst he was on duty, to paint a moon on one of his works without any real success. He never mentioned it.

Randall spent the main years of his boyhood in Longway in Chantry Lane:

> The most distinguishing feature of the house was a very steep staircase because the builder, according the family story, had forgotten to put it into the plans. The house stood in 1/3 of an acre, part of which was planted with apple trees. Father paid c. £600 for it. Part of the garden had been a tennis court but it was overgrown and we played football there. Often we would have a number of friends and some locals in the garden much to Father's horror although he never forbade the use of it as a playground. We had several second hand bikes, never a new one. One in particular was a racing type with wooden rimmed wheels which was bought by Father from a Mrs. Risborough whose son had been killed in the war. We played games of make-believe, football on bikes, circus acts standing on the seats and holding handlebars. We did trick riding with two or three on one bike and putting handkerchiefs on sticks and riding as fast as we could and picking them off. After Father took me up to Cuffley to see the start of an air race to somewhere in the north, we were inspired to pretend that our bikes were airplanes by fixing wooden propellers on the front.
> Originally chalk had been excavated nearby and the house stood higher than the remainder of the ground. The dells were not very deep but we would race up and down them. Very occasionally mischief crept in such as racing close to the old road cleaner and knocking off his hat. Shame really for he was a dear old man. Father bought a Hansom cab from Oliver Berry, general manager of the Great Northern railway at Roe Hill House, which stood by the waterworks in Chantry lane and put it in the garden. We

had many happy days of make-believe in and on that carriage.

The house adjoined Roe Green Farm South and a footpath ran down the side of Mr. White's field. This we used to get to the railway station at Nast Hyde Halt to go to St Albans. We four children became very friendly with the farmer and his men and Roly and I would help with harvest, hay time and potato picking. We enjoyed this especially when we rode home on the backs of the horses at the end of the day. The horses seemed very tall to we small boys but they were very docile. I did a week's potato picking one holiday. For this I received £1.00 my first ever wage. On receipt of this on the Friday evening I went down to the Old Fiddle with aching back and consoled myself by buying 12 penny bars of Sharp's Creamy toffee which I ate at one go. How sick I was.

The travelling groom and stallion was another event during the year. Farmers were advised of a visit to the district of a stallion. If they had a mare and they wished to breed from her the groom would bring the stallion to the farm. The groom and horse were dressed up for the occasion. The groom would be smart in his cap, suit and polished leggings with his belongings in a roll on the front of his saddle. The horse was brushed and shining with a decorated mane. Often the two would make "calls" over 12 – 20 miles in a day.

Father was a special constable during WWI and on three nights a week at 10pm a policeman, Mr. Carter called for him and after a glass of beer they set off to the waterworks at the top of the hill to see there was no damage or sabotage. Mr. Isaacs, who was in charge of the waterworks, lived on the site and no doubt he entertained the two of them at night. Mr. Isaacs mode of transport was a two wheeled cart pulled by a mule. Most of the local horses had been commandeered by the military. I don't recall that any incident happened although bombs fell in the area, being dropped from zeppelins. The most awesome sight was seeing a German airship which had been attacked by a British plane in flames one night[23]. It crashed in a field near Potters Bar. My mother got Roly and me out of bed to see it.

The farms in Roe Green provided much interest and space for us to roam and play games in the fields around. Ponds provided entertainment when we went fishing for tiddlers and frogspawn. More than once we were chased off by the farmer.

After the end of the war some horses came back to the farm. My Father had a cavalry bugle – goodness knows where he got it from – and to amuse us he would take us to the field where they were and blow a bugle call and the horses would line up and gallop down the field. I doubt if it gave them happy memories.

The bugle was hung on the wall of my grandparents' house when I was small. Sometimes Gran Tingey would let us take it down and we would blow through the dirty brass mouthpiece. We could never get a peep out of it. My father also remembered that:

> One memorable day a stag came running down the next field to the house followed by dogs and huntsmen. The poor thing jumped into the pond opposite White's Farm and was dragged out and taken away in a van. I never liked hunting after that. We would watch when the steam engines came for the ploughing. There were two, one at each side of the field. Attached to each was a drum which

---

[23] This was probably the German *airship* SL 11 which was shot down and crashed in *Cuffley* on 3 September 1916 part of an intended aerial bombardment of London.

held a wire hawser. This was hooked on to the plough and the engines pulled the plough back and forth across the field. Looking back to those days I realise we were very fortunate to have such freedom and simple pleasures.

Once, at least, and probably in 1925, the long summer holidays were enhanced by a week in Skegness. There is a snapshot of Emilie with her four children and Mr and Mrs Simmons with their son, Reg – Randall's best friend. There they sit on the beach formally dressed and somewhat solemn.

Why Skegness with its reputation for being bracing? The reason must be because there were special trains from King's Cross in the summer which stopped in Hatfield. It must have been the furthest trip from home that any of the children had experienced.

There was no school in Roe Green and Randall was enrolled at Countess Anne's School in old Hatfield in 1913 when he was five years old. He recalled:

> I caused my mother a lot of trouble by being very reluctant to attend and was often taken to school by her in a pushchair. One vivid memory I have is of arriving at about 10.00am (via pushchair) and being made to stand "in the corner" by Mrs. Harbour, the teacher – which did not make me any keener to attend. On another occasion, when the medical officer attended school, I was sent home with a message: "Tell your mother your garters are too tight." I have very little remembrance of being taught anything. When I think about it now I'm ashamed of the trouble I gave mother. It was a walk of 1½ miles each way from Longway.

The younger boys also went to Countess Anne's but Joan went straight to Alexandra House, a small private school on the old Great North Road. She did not start until she was seven because of the distance to be walked - four times a day because there were no school dinners. Presumably Emilie was tired of escorting her children by then.

Alexandra House was a sister school to Dagmar House, next door. This was originally a boarding school "for young gentlemen" started in Hatfield around 1870 and moved to a site on the Old Great North Road. The three Tingey boys and their cousins all attended as day boys. Randall recounted:

> I started in the Infants' Class at six years old. I have very vague memories of this, apart from being given a bar of chocolate for spelling the word CHOCOLATE correctly. Later I went into the Boys' school proper. Father paid £3 per term. I was a day boy, so walked home to dinner at Roe Green in between twelve noon and two o'clock. The school day opened with prayers. Homework was usual. There was often school on Saturday mornings. I played cricket, tennis, football and fives. PE consisted of a little

gymnastics but was chiefly drill and marching. Our PE Instructor was Sergeant Panter. Being wartime for my first four years there, we were drilled in military fashion. At break we played marbles or fag cards.
We were divided into four houses: York, Lancaster, Tudor and Stuart. There was much rivalry between the Houses. A master was in charge of each House and a boy was captain. I was captain of Tudor later on. I played all the aforesaid mentioned games for the House and was in the school football team from the age of eleven until I left at sixteen. I passed seven or eight subjects in the Oxford and Cambridge Junior Certificate. The masters I remember were: the Head, John Dare, strict but very fair and gentlemanly; Lishmann who was very severe and carried a cane up his sleeve. He wore a frock coat and pin-stripe trousers and smelled of beer at times. Sladen, the housemaster of Tudor was a sporty type. M. Buisseret was the French teacher. Kevin, who taught chemistry, was a dear but had no discipline. There were, of course, others over the ten years I was there. Looking back I feel that I suffered from lack of confidence but I have no regrets about my schooldays.

His cousin, Eric, who also went to Dagmar, was less content with his education there:

It was a terrible school, really archaic. In our main class room the desks were kitchen tables and we had forms to sit on. It was in a dreadful situation with the trains roaring past at the back all the time and the standard of education was very poor. I suppose our fathers thought they were doing the best by us sending us to a private school but I think we would have got a better education at St Audrey's, the local state school.

Randall enjoyed reading. Several of his books by Henty, Jack London, Kingsley and Marryat, sometimes won as prizes, became favourites of mine. He carefully listed those he had been lent and a few which he had loaned to others in a pocket notebook.

Football was his favourite leisure occupation. In the notebook that his mother gave him in 1920 he listed players and results in national and many local teams. He was also interested in cricket, recording the scores of well-known cricketers in his notebook, along with some records of Air races. Interspersed in his notebook were more homely comments like:

> I won third prize in our sports in the 100 yards. It was a good writing case".
>
> Jan 2nd 1922. We had a good game of footer up the Common in the morning which resulted in a draw 6-6. I scored 1. Roly played a fine game.

He went on to play for the Pirates – a youth club in the town. This club provided a variety of sports and entertainment for the local teenagers. They met in the Reading room at Newtown and sometimes there was a little horseplay when gas mantles got smashed or a window broken and once they broke a chair or two while playing football indoors. But, said Randall,

> We were not really rough, just a bit wild. There was a hockey section and a football team. Our colours were blue shirt, white shorts and red stockings. We played in the mid-Herts league for a number of seasons.

As in so many small family businesses the children were expected to help from an early age. On Sunday mornings Randall and Roly used to go into Newtown, collect the horse, ride it round the lanes to Longway, let it graze on the lawn then take it home. In the holidays he, and often his cousin Eric, would go out with Albert Cannon, the roundsman, who was known as Diggler, to deliver goods. Albert was a tubby little man who wore a flat cap, grey overalls and smoked a short pipe which in wet weather he smoked bowl down. He taught the boys to smoke with shag rolled in newspaper under the canvas cover of the cart. He told tall stories: that there were lions and tigers in the woods around Colney Heath and was so convincing that they weren't sure if this was fact or fiction. One young friend, Gerald Scott, was so frightened on his first journey with Diggler that he never went again. Diggler was a practical joker and would send the boys on footling errands: "Go and ask Mr. Streader for a square peg for this hole in the barrel".

When I was a child he was still working as our warehouseman: "What've you been doing, Diggler?" I asked. "I've been washing the coals, m'dear." With doubtful curiosity I trotted round to the heap next to the garden shed to see if the coal was gleaming and clean.

In 1924 when he was sixteen Randall started full-time work in the shop. There was no discussion about any other career. He had already begun to do the accounts for his father in the evenings before he left school. His wage of 5/- a week was the same as that of my mother when she started her apprenticeship though I believe that her experiences were happier than my father's early days in the business. But he can speak for himself.

> The business had continued to flourish and there was a staff of men and boys, Orders were collected by men, two and sometimes three of whom used cycles to collect the orders which were often delivered the same day. When I joined the firm we still used a horse and cart for deliveries. The front part of the horse's stable was used as store house for bulk goods. Being a wooden building it

was susceptible to infestations of rats and mice. I hated visiting the store in darkness, usually with a hurricane lamp, for on opening the door there was a scurry of small feet.

At the rear of the shop was a shed in which paraffin, large casks of treacle and sacks of soda were kept. Treacle in cold weather was reluctant to leave the cask via a brass tap and occasionally one was tempted to leave it for a minute or so to trickle into the container. This could be catastrophic as I myself knew, for one evening a friend called me from the open door to fix arrangements for a football match. We got talking and I completely forgot and when I returned part of the floor was covered around two inches deep in treacle. The only way to clean this up was to get a sack of wood shavings from Streaders, tip it on to the treacle and after a while shovel the whole mess up and dispose of it on waste ground which was within easy distance. That I had to do before I went home to supper. And I had not been the first to forget. Several years before Harry Ewington had locked up the shop at night and came back next morning to find a lake of treacle over the whole yard. He reckoned he was lucky not to get the sack.

Dried fruit, currants and sultanas were also kept in the shed and we had to clean them. A wooden cask, which had arrived from a supplier with assorted goods packed in straw or hay, would have a wire sieve placed on top and a quantity of the fruit would be placed in the sieve and sprinkled with water. Then with both hands one would proceed to rub the fruit in a circular manner so that the grit and grime fell through. On a cold winter night before Christmas this was not an enviable task.

The paraffin was delivered by Anglo-American Oil Co. St Albans Depot in 5 or 10 gallon cans and tipped into the

500 gallon tank. Salt was also stored in the shed, it being bought in 28lb blocks and sawn with a zinc saw into a number of penny bars according to the cost of the block.

As business expanded we had to rent a cellar at the rear of the Boar and Castle for the storage of cheese, butter and bacon. To get these items into the cellar one had to borrow from the pub the slide on which barrels of beer were lowered. Many a time the cellar was flooded and panic ensued. The goods had to be lifted on to empty wooden crates. At night in the winter the only means of light was a hurricane lantern.

Eggs for sale were collected from farms or brought in by customers who kept hens. As soon as I could drive I drove a Ford van around Symonds Hyde and Coleman Green delivering orders and collecting eggs which were placed in hay lined boxes. The price agreed was usually determined by the price of eggs at Hertford market.

Many of the local customers came into the shop every day buying whatever they needed for their meal that night or even a 1d of sugar. Their purchases were recorded in a large ledger and the total was paid at the end of the week. Most people paid regularly. Dad would say it was often those with more money that were slack at paying their bills. I remember Kate Bunyan who lived in a small cottage in the fifth Right of Way would come in punctually at 10.30am every Friday. "What do I owe yer, Mr. Tingey?" she would pipe. Kate was a tiny little woman with a very large husband whom she ruled with a rod of iron. Some days she would come into the shop twice for a pennyworth of tea. My father would pull her leg. If she were to go on complaining about her husband Father would say "What did you do, Kate? Hammer his knees till he fell?" And she would laugh, lift up her apron and scurry out of the shop.

A few of the "carriage trade" customers would telephone their orders. We had one of the early telephones – Hatfield 40. I was scared to use it and if it rang I would slip upstairs into a stockroom. Eventually Harry Ewington – who had previously worked at with us but went to the furniture shop with Edmund Thomas, was determined to get me to get over my fright. He would ring and ask for me by name forcing me to come down and reply.

J.E. died in May 1924[24] and John Tingey was now in sole ownership of the grocery business. Nine years previously Tom had bought Rye farm at Eaton Bray near Dunstable at auction. The plan was that his brother, John, then aged thirty-five would run it. The two brothers got on very well, but Tom probably thought that the two would make a better living apart. After all, his elder son Eric was within a few years of joining the business and John had three sons. However, though John was keen, Emilie could not persuade herself to be a farmer's wife "with cows just outside the window". John employed a manager and kept the farm for a time. Randall remembered going over at weekends by train with his father and younger brother. After three or four years, however, John sold the farm and his future was firmly back in the shop.

By this time, however, Tom had moved on. He suggested that the business should be split. He had always been more interested in the furniture so he decided to build his own premises and develop that side of the business. In 1919 he had gone to the bank, secured a loan, and built the Corner House, which was quickly dubbed Tingey's Emporium by locals.

After J.E.'s death John bought Rose Cottage from Jess and Ruth for it had been left to them by their father. Brother

---

[24] His funeral conducted by J.J. Burgess & Sons who did the same for three generations of the Tingey family – always with consummate dignity and thoughtful kindness.

Tom had a house built for them next to his own new shop and there they lived for the rest of their lives. John, Emilie and the family left Longway and moved in. It was conveniently near to the shop though it had drawbacks. Joan, the one daughter, said:

> There was a bath upstairs but no water laid on and traipsing up and down with water caused Mother to have a hernia. It was a large house. I can remember waking up in the night and seeing spiders on the wall. Norman and I shared a bedroom which would be frowned upon today.

They settled in. Roland, Norman and Joan walked to school, now less than a mile away. Randall and his father went up the road to the shop at 7.30 in the morning.

Randall had been working for a year when he first saw Florrie in the shop but it was not love at first sight with him. He did not remember that first meeting. As you will find out, the matchmaking was all hers – to the lasting benefit of them both.

Chapter 4

Work and Play

My mother's heroines were Florence Nightingale and Edith Cavell. She had dreamed of training to be a nurse when she left school but felt it would be unkind to leave her mother. Mind you, in later years she said percipiently "I would have liked to be a nurse but I think I would have wanted to start as a Sister." Her granddaughter Kate, aged six in 1969, also thought about nursing as a career but an item in Blue Peter stopped her in her tracks: "I shan't be a nurse after all. I'll have to find another career," she said regretfully. "They are not going to wear cloaks any more. They are not even going to have caps or belts - not even aprons."

Neither the attractiveness of the uniform nor the feminist determination to choose a career affected her grandmother. In 1925, having had no opportunity to obtain any qualifications, a "career" was not an option. Luckily what she did was exactly right for her. It provided an inspiration for her subsequent and considerable skill with the needle, developed her ability as a saleswoman and enhanced her confidence. Indeed so lasting was her pleasure in her employment before her marriage that at eighty-six years old she wrote a vivid article about it. The Lady magazine published it and she was proud and delighted to receive £150.00.

I reproduce it here with some additions.

SPARY & HOLLIDAY
Reminiscences of a St. Albans dress shop 1926 - 1933.[25]

"A plain brown dress with a white collar would do very well. I'll let you know within the week."
In 1926 I was sixteen years old. I had been apprenticed for nine months to Miss Day-Brown, a dressmaker in St Albans, Hertfordshire. I had learned a lot about needlework but I was too young to settle down alone to needle and thread and I was easily distracted. The boys of the Abbey school passing by the window were one regular distraction. Miss Day Brown tried to vary my day and sent me out to deliver accounts and walk her Bedlington terrier while I was doing it. This dog was a mad creature. Once, when he was awoken from sleep by a loud noise outside the window of the workroom, he jumped straight through the plate glass. I was horribly embarrassed when I was walking him one day. He tried to relieve his bowels and out came a long remnant of material. Unable to rid himself of it he began to snap and growl at it. Finally I had to take him to a quiet spot, put one foot on the end of the material and pull him away from it. Miss Day Brown thought it funny. I didn't at the time. Eventually Miss Day-Brown told my mother that she thought I would be happier working amongst people.
At this time my Aunt Florrie was staying with us. One morning, she passed Spary & Holliday's, a smart dress shop in Market Street, where a notice in the window said "Apprentice wanted".
I began a five year apprenticeship on five shillings a week with an occasional bonus. I was allowed one week's holiday in the spring and two weeks in the summer plus

---

[25] With grateful acknowledgement to The Lady magazine. Article published July 21, 1998

Christmas and Boxing Day. For Christmas I was allowed thirty shillings in value of goods in the shop. Since a good coat then cost about £2.00 and a nice dress might sell for 19/11d, this was a useful bonus. When I was twenty-one, engaged and out of apprenticeship, my wages were 30/- plus 3d in the £ commission on all that I sold.

Working hours were 8.30 am till 6.00pm, 8.00pm on Saturdays. We had an hour and a quarter for lunch and a fifteen minute tea break was allowed morning and afternoon. Thursday was early closing in St Albans so that was our afternoon off.

The shop was owned by two ladies. Miss Spary was a tall angular woman with a pleasing deep voice and a most attractive laugh. She had long black hair drawn into a tight bun and kind brown eyes. I grew to adore her. Her partner, Miss Holliday, was a poor thing; a fair haired, fluffy type of person, who always spent one day a week in bed to keep up her strength. Miss Holliday did the accounts. When I started work with them they lived above the shop. Miss Holliday's mother lived with them, a tall and autocratic lady rather like Queen Mary. She spent a lot of time seated at a pianola, no doubt thinking she was playing it. The staff did not like her, believing that she was a drag on the real bread winner, Miss Spary. After Mrs. Holliday died the two ladies decided to move into a house. Our accounts went out quarterly and the local ones were delivered by hand. If we were not busy in the morning Nell and I enjoyed the outings. One morning Miss Spary said "Look out for a nice house for us, Florence." The result was that we saw just the right house in Carlisle Avenue. They moved and stayed there for the rest of their lives.

The girls working at the shop were all older than I. There was Lily Syms, a sharp, dark haired young lady; Nell

Hing was a complete contrast, fair and uncertain of herself. She had to be called Mildred in the showroom because "Nell" was considered unsuitable. Later, a Miss Higgs, known to us as Higgy joined the staff. I, of course, was Florence, though the girls always called me Bobby. We all became good friends friends that I kept up with for the rest of their lives. When I indulge in a cream cake I sometimes think of the birthdays at the shop. The birthday girl had to go out to Buglers in the town and buy cakes for all of us: I always used to buy cream puffs, the choux pastry so crisp that you could break off little pieces and dip them into the rich cream.

There was also a small squat man who used to clean and sweep outside. He used to take goods on approval to customers, carrying them in a light wooden box with leather strappings. Jennie the maid, lived in a small room upstairs. She cleaned both house and shop and did the cooking. It must have been a lonely life for her. She loved to talk to us when she got the chance. There was a small fitting room and, towards the back of the shop, a room where the dressmakers, Mrs. Garner, Miss Peters and later Miss Turner did alterations.

Our cloakroom was upstairs on a mezzanine floor above the fitting room. The door of the W.C. had a lock on both sides. One morning when Higgy was passing she saw the door was slightly open and automatically locked it. Miss Spary, who had gone up to the stockroom at 9.30am did not reappear. At 11.00am Miss Holliday looked for her and let her out of the lavatory. Was Higgy's face red!

The shop was on a corner with display windows on three sides of the building. One side led to an alleyway at the back of the Town Hall. Beneath the Town Hall were the cells where the prisoners were kept on Court day. This caused us some excitement as we watched from the kitchen window during our morning break. Inside the shop two glass countered cases held ornamental trays, displaying scarves, lace jabots and fichus[26]. Pure silk stockings were priced at 4/11d and art silk pairs at 1/11d.

Miss Spary had started her working life as a shop assistant. Life had not been smooth for her. When I was much older she once told me that when she left work at perhaps ten o'clock on a Saturday evening to return to her home in Markyate on her bicycle – almost nine miles away - she would be so tired that only by dint of pedalling from one telegraph post to the next could she get herself home. When she arrived it was often to find a brother in a drunken state who had been sick all over the floor and furniture.

She rose to be head of the dress department at Greens, a high class department store in St Albans, before she began her own business and she was an excellent saleswoman. Her methods were somewhat unorthodox. I have seen her display a gown with a swish, covering the price ticket with one hand and quoting a price twice as high. The customer was a lady who would not have looked at the garment if she had known the lower price.

Another customer used to come into the shop and select about a dozen dresses. Then Miss Spary and I used to take them to her house. We were highly embarrassed on one visit for, as the customer pulled a dress over her head, her wig came off with it and she was completely bald.

One customer always caused great mirth for she was a sweet old lady with badly fitting dentures which caused her to whistle as she pronounced certain words. We would wait for the noise, trying to suppress our giggles. Another regular customer always had her two daughters' shantung dresses for college made by one of our dressmakers. We

---

[26] Lacy collars and small shawls

were always interested in these girls, for one was pretty and the other so very plain and gawky though she had a charming manner rather like Joyce Grenfell.

The fitting room was near a covered rail where garments were hung which were going to the dressmakers for alterations. Miss Spary also kept her outdoor coat there. One day, from the fitting room, a young lady saw a nicely patterned tweed sleeve, pulled out the coat and tried it on. It needed shortening. Nothing daunted, Miss Spary had it altered and sold her own coat. In due course the girl brought the coat back. She was sure Miss Spary was unaware that the coat was stained under the arms. We never saw that coat again.

We had two wax models in the shop which were nicknamed Georgina and Esmeralda. One day Miss Spary was serving a wealthy customer and her two daughters. The girls were wandering round the showroom and Miss Spary was excited at the quantity of clothes that were being bought. In trying to move one of the models, which meant placing both hands each side of its "hips" she picked up one of the girls instead. Effusive apologies were made and no damage done to the sales but, when the customers had left, Miss Spary and the staff collapsed in laughter. Between chuckles Miss Spary managed to say, "When I felt her soft warm botty, I thought the stand had melted."

Georgina and Esmeralda were always dressed in garments suitable for the time of day. On Saturday evenings, at six o'clock, we cleared the two narrow windows, one of which could be seen in the market place, the other along the alleyway. While outside in the market the traders, their stalls lit with oil lamps, were selling off their goods cheaply, our two wax models made a sudden and dramatic reappearance, dressed in evening gowns with full accessories - bags, scarves and brooches. People were drawn to look by Miss Spary's showmanship.

Market Day itself always provided some excitement: Buck Lawrence had a stall just outside the shop door. It was a box on legs and he sold rabbits – yelling out his wares. I thought it was interesting to watch him shouting and skinning his rabbits. Every time he popped out the eyes with his thumb he gave a little click of the tongue. Buck was a short stumpy man with a red snuffly nose whereas his brother with whom he ran a rag and bone business during the week, was tall, thin and weedy. Miss Spary did not like Buck so close to her high class dress establishment, so one Saturday she said "Come along, Florence, help me to move that stall whilst that man is at dinner" and we did.

We were not expected to let a customer leave the shop without buying something and we were never allowed to be idle. Miss Spary would muddle the trays and drawers so that we could look busy as we tidied them up. Winter was very hard as no heat was allowed in the showroom (being bad for the dresses). We all had chilblains and I remember counting ten on my fingers. We were allowed to wear black mittens.

Miss Spary went to Paris every spring to buy dresses. When the fashion was for short, scant dresses made of sequins, the dresses arrived in tea chests lined with black paper. The dresses were heavy and ran through our hands like a string of beads or chain mail.

Every spring Nell and I had a lovely job packing a trunk for a lady who lived at Bourne End. This lady went for a cruise each spring. First she was fitted out with day and evening dresses, underwear and hosiery. Then she sent to the shop all her shoes and other items and, with mountains of tissue paper, Nell and I packed - and dreamed. She always sent us a present to thank us for the excellent packing.

Miss Spary also went on a foreign holiday every spring. She used to ask me to take her strong box to the bank. One time the clerk said "Your mother on her travels again?"

"She's not my mother"

"Well, she always says 'I'll send my little girl in.'"

One year she went to Egypt, bringing back photographs of her party with camels in the desert. For the first time I realised the desert was not flat. The ladies in Egypt do not look as if they had let themselves go at all - and what hot clothes for that climate.

It was always hard to pin Miss Spary down about our own holidays. The others used to say "You ask her, Florence. She'll listen to you." I did and she would say reprovingly, "You know, Florence, the others are senior to you."

We had high jinks when she was away. Who could walk up three flights of stairs with a roll of black georgette on her head and draped around the body? There was a standing three panelled mirror which stood on legs and great fun was had by trying to wriggle underneath without toppling the whole mirror.

We girls used to pair off at lunchtime. Nell and I were the romantic ones. In slack times we hugged the radiators and wrote love stories. When I was sixteen she caused me to write myself a letter saying, "Do you remember Randall Tingey?" and put it in an envelope marked, "Open this when you are twenty-one."[27]

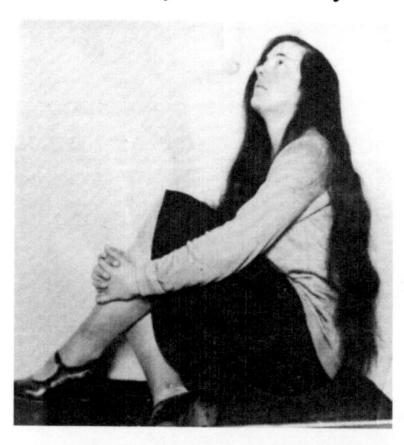

Sometimes we girls at the shop would go out together on our half day. In the summer of 1930 we often used to take a picnic down to Verulamium in order to see how the archaeological excavations of the Roman city were progressing. At that time the site of the lake was being dug out and Mortimer Wheeler was in charge of the excavations. We were allowed to go very close to the dig. A few times, under supervision, I was even allowed to wield a brush, very gently, to clear soil from a piece of wall or a fragment of pot. I remember that the steps to the medieval wine cellar were discovered in the field leading from where the monks came from the Abbey to the Fighting Cocks, yet no mention is ever made of them. I can't have imagined it, can I?

I used to go home for lunch, usually walking one way and catching a bus back. Living in Fleetville nearly two miles away it must have taken me about half an hour. My

---

[27] She did – see next chapter. And, what is more it is still in my mother's effects: a tired little envelope which, on the outside says: Remember and Open 21st June 1931. Inside, on the top of a Spary and Holliday bill heading there is written in faded brown ink: Remember Randall Tingey of Rose Cottage, Hatfield – your friend. Written 21st June 1926.

mother and I had a light lunch and ate properly in the evening. However, on Thursday afternoons, my half-day, my mother would always have a special dinner ready for me with such treats as stuffed lambs' hearts or undercut of steak in batter followed by apple dumplings. Then off to No Man's land with Sybil and Madge to pick blackberries. Home to tea:bread and butter, blackberry jam and Mother's cake. Then Madge and I went off to meet the boys.

Two sisters, the Misses Fish, were customers who lived in a large house which was on my route. They could not have been at all interested in clothes, for they always wore black Edwardian suits that were brown, almost green with age, the skirts brushing the pavement and just revealing their black, buttoned boots. They did however buy our lace jabots - stiff lace collars with rows of pleated lace descending to the chest. They would come up Market Street one behind the other. The first was very upright and walked with a martial step, carrying her parasol rigidly above her head; her sister who was very bent, scuttled behind using her stick very much as an aid to walking. Having each chosen a jabot they would ask to have them delivered on "appro" - approval - and I would take them to their house on my way to lunch.

We had another customer who lived two miles beyond my home, and she too liked to have items on approval. She seemed to take a fancy to me, calling me her 'little ray of sunshine'. She was a young married woman and I suspect now that she must have been lonely. The first time I went to her house one summer evening after work, she suggested that we went into the garden for a game of badminton. Then she made us tea. Consequently I arrived home very late for my own supper, quite worrying my mother. I described the episode to Miss Spary the next day and thereafter, whenever the "Little Ray of Sunshine" was asked for, I was sent home to lunch with the instruction that I need not bother to go back to work.

Though I had thick long hair I wanted to be in fashion and have it in "earphones" or bobbed. I decided to have it cut when on holiday. Miss Spary didn't like it, but after a while all the other assistants had their hair bobbed. For weeks they all felt uncomfortable feeling her eyes on the back of their necks. Of course, later, she had her hair shingled, too.

Towards the end of my time at the shop she decided to learn to drive. She thought I knew all about driving as she knew that my "nice young friend, Randall" drove a car. What hair-raising times I had. We came out of the garage one day and Miss Spary unknowingly caught the bumper. Consequently we kangaroo-hopped up the London Road and into Chequers Street because the wheel was trapped in the bent bumper.

"Whatever is the matter, Florence? What shall we do?"
"We'd better stop," I said firmly. She had lessons after that. One day she asked the instructor if he had taught anyone worse than her. His reply was "One, and he gave up". He said that Miss Spary was the only pupil he had that tried to turn on a main road.

Soon after I married in 1933 Miss Spary told me that she and Miss Holliday were retiring and selling the business to the three assistants. "It's not the same now you've gone," she said. My three maiden lady colleagues had no thought of marriage when I was wed, yet Lily met Ted on holiday and was married two years later and Nell married David Ewer, from her church. Towards the end of life at Spary's, Saturday evenings had been enlivened by seeing a man looking in the side windows as we were dressing them. This happened every week. The rest of us were sure that he was looking at Higgy. Eventually he would smile and touch his hat. Finally he met her outside the shop and asked to keep company with her and she eventually married him in 1938. Spary & Holliday's was no more.

My father was perhaps not so lucky in his work. He told he had never speculated on what he would have liked to have done – though it was said by one football manager that he could have made a career in professional football. He was too diffident to enjoy selling, too quiet for the cut and thrust of business. He once said that he thought that he might like to have been a postman. Another dream was that in retirement he thought he would have liked to live on a Scottish Croft for a year – just to see if he could. But though not an entrepreneur, he was conscientious, honest and careful, with a good head for figures – not bad qualities in a shopkeeper.

It was unlikely that he would be forward in love. What luck it was that his future wife could make all the going.

****

"How old were you when you got your first Valentine's card?" I asked my mother wistfully in February 1949, when I was thirteen and there was no likelihood that such a card would arrive for me in the post.

She stopped rolling pastry for a moment and smiled reminiscently.

"Well, I don't remember when I first got a card, but I certainly remember the first time I sent one. Three of us were in Mrs. Blakley's little corner shop in Fleetville picking over the cards and I found one that showed a monk in a brown habit with an arrow in his bottom and Cupid looking round the corner. It was entitled "Rotten shot!" And Madge said to me," Peggy, I dare you to send that on Valentine's Day to that boy you met in your friend's village." So I did.

"But your name's not Peggy" I objected.

"No, but we had a club and we were all named after some girls in a school story - by Angela Brazil, I think. I was Peggy, Cath was Miriam and Madge was…well, I forget who Madge was. But anyway, you know how I hated my real names: Florence Daisy! Who wanted to be called that?"

Quite a lot of girls now in the twenty first century I guess, but a hundred years ago they obviously weren't popular – certainly not with her. Perhaps that is why my mother gathered so many nicknames as she went along in life: Peggy as a girl; Hopey or Bobby, (after the film star, Bob Hope) when she was at work. She and my father called each other "Dall" – from Randall. My brother as a teenager rebelled at "Mummy" and invented Mog. And that stuck, although our daughter, Kate, couldn't manage Gran and so she and her sister, Nell, had Dan and Dar for their maternal grandparents. Her own mother, my Gran Hope, always called her "Florrie". Since now I always think of her as Mog that is how I'll call her from now on. And if "Pop" sometimes occurs in the narrative it is the name my father acquired later in life.

Some people seem to collect nicknames. Are they characters who excite affection, amusement? Do nicknames indicate that the person has a good circle of friends? You can judge if it was so with Mog.

"How old were you?" And was it Daddy you sent it to?" I asked with some concern. Had some other boy had taken Mog's fancy? And Mog regaled me with the story that I daresay I had heard before, and one that she told her grandchildren many years later.

She was fourteen in 1924 but she pinpointed that card as the beginning of her love life. When René's mother had said "There are two nice boys in the grocery shop at Hatfield", they did not take any persuading:

I stood at the counter near the taller boy. He was quiet and only spoke to Mrs. Payne. While we were there he lit the gas lamp and dropped the match which fell on my hand. I hoped he did it on purpose but I doubt it. As we walked away from the shop René said "I'll have the tall one and you can have the other," but I said silently to myself, "Oh, no you won't."

This story is all hers and takes us up to 1933. However, excited by her success with the account of Spary & Holliday, she composed a second article two years later when she was eighty- eight. Sadly The Lady rejected this much to her disappointment. Was it too salacious?

COURTSHIP – A FORGOTTEN ART

After that first visit to the grocers' shop in Hatfield, René and I badgered Mrs. Payne to find out more about the two boys we had seen. We soon learned that the tall one was the son of John Tingey, the grocer, and was called Randall - his mother's maiden name. His friend was Bob Cannon, son of the landlord of The Gun Inn.
We did not see them again for many months but one fine evening when I was fifteen my other good friend, Madge, and I decided to go for a walk and we strolled along the road from Fleetville to Oaklands where there were woods and trees to climb. We enjoyed this and walked that way several times that summer. One evening the same two boys passed on a motorbike on their way to St Albans. We were quite excited and hopefully walked to the woods each evening. The boys often came that way and sometimes they stopped and sat on a farm gate. They knew we were in the woods but were apparently too shy to speak to us. Madge and I decided this couldn't go on so

we worked out a plan.

We would go into the woods and Madge would climb a tree then pretend she couldn't get down. This we did. I started for home in the gathering dusk. Madge yelled. I passed the boys and one said, "What's the matter?"

I, all indignant, said "She's making out she can't get down."

"We'll go and help her" they said.

The ice was broken. We had many happy evenings in the woods after that. We even built a tree house, sitting and talking for hours. It was all very innocent.

One evening when they came, Randall looked pale and unwell. He and I walked in the woods and he was sick. We were both embarrassed. I learned later from Bob that he had jaundice, so we didn't see the boys for a few weeks. By this time I had left school and was apprentice in the dress shop. It was then that Nell suggested that I wrote a note to myself saying "Do you remember Randall Tingey, your friend? June 21, 1926. Open in five years' time".

As winter approached the boys came in the family car. Madge and I would walk along the road and sometimes we could see the headlights shafting through the night sky - there were not many cars in those days. This was high glee. On fine evenings we walked to the local farm and leaned on the farm gate chatting. One night the farmer, a mean old man, removed the top hinges so when we leaned on the gate all four of us fell to the ground in a heap.

During the winter on Thursday evenings we went to The Grand Palace, a cinema in St. Albans. This became a regular outing. Randall always stopped at the sweet shop for half a pound of Cadbury's shapes. I got fed up with these. Madge and I used to giggle when, while hoping they were different chocolates, we saw the same old ones.

One evening, coming out of the cinema, we met my mother coming home from the Adult school. We introduced the boys and then my mother said "I wish you wouldn't keep my daughter out so late." I could have killed her.

Randall was a shy young man, but eventually he asked me to go for a ride on his prized Norton motorbike. So one Sunday morning he arrived at our house. Of course my brother, Ben, was interested in the bike and Randall seemed happy in our family and came again. My mother thought he was "a nice young man". Eventually I went to Hatfield one afternoon because Ran had acquired a Morgan car of which he was very proud and we cleaned it together. Mrs. Tingey called us in for tea, so another hurdle was cleared. By 1927 we seemed to have become a couple and enjoyed so many happy times together.

Dunstable Downs was our favourite place for walking and we would go there on our half days off. I have a photo of me there in a flowered print that Ran always liked. There was very little kissing but we became good friends.

What were the attractions that gradually cemented the lifelong partnership? Randall must have been attracted to Mog's vivacity and friendliness, and he loved her glossy chestnut hair. He was upset when she had it shingled. And Mog told me that he liked her legs. Good shapely ones they were, formed no doubt from energetic playing of netball. And Mog saw a tall, fair young man who, behind the shyness, was thoughtful, had a lurking sense of fun and perhaps, though lacking confidence, had some assurance that an established large extended family had given him. By the time Mog was eighteen the relationship had grown close:

> When my mother and I went to Battle Abbey for a holiday in 1928 I wrote to Ran every day - a pile of letters which he and I burned at the beginning of World War II in case they were blown to the winds in the bombing and found by prying eyes.
> In 1930 Mrs. Tingey was in hospital having had a serious operation. Although the family had help in the day time, evening cover was a problem. Joan, Randall's sister, was only fourteen years old so with the three boys and father it was quite a houseful. I often went over after leaving work. I remember cooking two pounds of sausages on a gas ring for Saturday night supper. When Mrs. Tingey came home I still went and stayed until the last bus at ten o'clock. Why didn't Randall take me home? Goodness knows!
> Randall and I went to Eastbourne for a holiday in the summer of 1930. The guest house had been recommended to us by one of our neighbours - a most superior lady - otherwise my mother would never have agreed to it. However, it turned out to be second rate and we were most embarrassed because one of the bedrooms was also our sitting room. Of course, we never thought of making use of the bed.
> In the autumn of that year he had to go into a London hospital and I did not see him for over two weeks. I played *Can't help loving 'dat man of mine* from *Showboat* on Ben's gramophone until my mother implored me to stop.

At Christmas 1930 everybody thought we would announce our engagement but I asked Ran to wait until June 21st, 1931 when I would open my letter to myself of five years before. That evening we went on one of our favourite walks down Tramp Dick[28] Lane and opened the letter. This was far more romantic than when Ran who, asking me to marry him, said "I suppose you better have a ring" Mind, he did know I didn't like rings.

We were married in October 1933 in St Etheldreda's in Old Hatfield. My wedding dress came from the shop where I worked. It was white georgette printed with sweet peas.

My gorgeous big bouquet was provided by Mr. Hall, the gardener at Hatfield House. It was a very quiet wedding. Ben gave me away, Rene and Joan were my bridesmaids.

The reception was at the

---

[28] Tramp Dick was a vagrant who lived in a rough wooden shack reinforced with sheets of corrugated iron. He wore old army boots and a brown coat tied round the middle with string. It was reputed that he came from a well-off family and went to Sandridge every week to get money from them. In the winter he used to break a few shop windows or steal potatoes and go to prison for a few weeks. Some children shouted at him and threw stones at the roof of his shed but others, including the Hope children would talk with him. At Christmas time Florrie and René used to take him a Christmas pudding which Gran Hope had cooked in a cloth specially for him.

Tingey's new house with just family and a few close friends. It was a quiet affair because Mrs. Tingey was still ill and not able to leave the house.

Why St Etheldreda's and Hatfield for the wedding? Gran Hope's church, which she attended regularly was at Fleetville. The surviving memorabilia of the wedding suggests co-operation and kindly thought. The invitations on cream deckled card were from Mrs. A.M Hope and Mrs. Tingey's ill-health was probably the main reason for the venue, but also the widowed Mrs. Hope living in a small rented terrace house, would have found it difficult to afford even a simple reception. Mog continued:

> We did not want to set off on our honeymoon that evening so Mrs. Tingey, having entered into our plans, left a bed and food for breakfast in the empty flat above the shop where we were going to set up home. We had planned to go to The Grand Palace after the reception but we overheard some of the others making up a party to see the same romantic film so we had to go to another cinema which was showing Laurel and Hardy! When it was over we drove back to Hatfield and put the car away as quietly as possible. We dare not put on any lights and crept about the flat with a torch, our giggles overcoming our shyness. In the morning we slipped off for our happy honeymoon at Mr. and Mrs. Shackle's at the White Rock, Hastings.
> When Randall died in 1991 we had enjoyed 57 years of happy marriage. It was not "a rotten shot" for us.

Perhaps the story is honed a little in the remembrance but it is a complete and happy tale. Their relationship did not bear out Deborah Kerr's aphorism: "A woman is lucky if she doesn't meet the right man before she is twenty-four."

Chapter 5

Before the War

It was strange not to have to go to work and it went to my head a bit. I used to read a lot of magazines and novels. I always enjoyed cooking our dinner and having it ready when Ran came up from the shop at lunch time but the housework became somewhat sketchy. I remember once after lunch when I had washed up and was just going to settle down with my book I noticed the front of our oak bureau. "I love you" read the message in the dust.

So wrote Mog, reflecting on the first months of her marriage. She was set firmly in Hatfield in 1933 and it is here that the rest of this story is played out. Her family had moved from Norfolk to Hemel Hempstead, to St Albans and Fleetville and the Tingeys journeyed from Royston to establish themselves in Hatfield. Unassuming and ordinary lives all of them, rising just a little in the world. From now on the story is that of my parents and very soon I will be in on the act, so what was the small stage on which we performed our parts before and during the World War II?

The flat above the shop where my parents set up home had been built only five years before. Randall's father, perhaps in emulation of his brother, had a fine new shop built in 1928 at a cost of £3000 on land which had previously been allotments on the south side of St Albans Road. Compared with all the little shops around, it would have seemed like a supermarket built in the middle of a High Street today. It was numbered 101 St Albans Road and we always referred to it by its number.

It surprises me that the family, not wild entrepreneurs, should have had the confidence to expand their business so dramatically in the years of uncertainty that began with the general strike of 1926 and were followed by economic depression. Nor do I remember any references to it when the family reminisced. Can't ask any of them now!

The new shop was a solid, unimaginative building. The first floor was of pebble-dash with brick ornamentation round the four sash windows on the frontage. The six plate-glass windows of the shop were surmounted by a board bearing the legend TINGEY & SONS on three sides, supplemented by GROCERY and PROVISIONS in smaller letters.

The interior of the shop was fitted with a long mahogany counter and had three stations separated by gleaming white Avery scales equipped with brass weights.

Assistants, in starched white aprons buttoned on to their crisp white jackets, waited on customers who sat on bentwood chairs placed beside heavy cast-iron radiators in front of the counters. A leisurely conversation would ensue while shopping lists were consulted and the items were assembled on the counter. Talk was punctuated by the noisy grinding of a red metal mill and the fragrant smell of fresh coffee would drift around the shop. A glass-fronted cabinet might be opened and a short ladder fetched to get Scott's Emulsion or other patent medicines from the topmost shelf. Paper bags were filled with biscuits from the stand in front of the counters where the tins were displayed and covered by glass topped and decorative lids.

Occasionally there would be an argument between customers' dogs, for there was no restriction on having them inside the shop on a lead. One memorable fracas occurred when the shop cat suddenly appeared on the counter and leapt upon the back of a dozing Alsatian. Howls and commotion ensued.

On the walls behind the grocery counters were shelves reaching to the high ceiling which contained packeted goods - there was a long pole to knock them in to the waiting hand of the assistant. Below them was the patent medicine cabinet, a bank of drawers for spices and metal lined pull-out bins with brass handles which held loose dry items like oats, lentils and beans and soft, brown sugar which was a solid mass of damp, crumbling grains. Under the counters were drawers containing many sizes and varieties of paper bags.

The provision counter across one end of the shop and the shelves behind it were made of white marble. These showed off the cheese and bacon and could be easily cleaned. Two red Berkel machines with gleaming steel cutters enabled the assistants to slice bacon in just the thickness of rasher desired. Cheese would be deftly cut to the customer's requirements with a fine wire fastened to a wooden dowel at each end. Butter packed into ¼ and ½ lb. blocks and wrapped in Tingey's own labels were stacked in neat piles on shelves. At Christmas whole hams would be displayed on stands and slices cut to order.

A space enclosed by dark wooden panelling at the opposite end from the provision counter formed an office. There was a chest-level slot where customers paid their bills. Inside, two polished leather topped desks held black ink stained ledgers with metal corners and red spines. The pages slumped heavily as the correct page was sought. The window was opaque to give privacy and a navy oiled silk blind could be pulled down against bright sunlight. The wide ledge at seat height tended to collect dead flies. A solid metal safe stood in one corner on which stood a stick telephone, the earpiece sometimes still damp from the previous user's ear.

On the day the shop was opened elaborate window displays were made, special price offers were a feature and Thorne's the millers gave away 1lb bags of flour. Tea and cakes were served to the customers and Randall's sister, Joan, aged twelve, found it all very exciting.

Provision for the staffs' needs was minimal. Behind the office and accessed by the passage leading to the yard were two dark, cramped cloakrooms smelling of carbolic soap and urine. A primitive gas ring and a small sink was the only place to make a hot drink. In my childhood they were cleaned by a lady known as Mrs. Mop who, fag in mouth, swished a lavatory brush down the pans, wiped the sinks and swilled the floor.

To the rear were a yard and a garage. Soon an enlarged dispatch room where orders were made up for delivery was added at the back of the shop. It had shelving at the back containing groceries and in the middle two long wooden benches, scrubbed every Saturday afternoon, were pushed together. Two or three assistants on one side assembled orders which were then passed over and checked for accuracy. On shelves beneath the bench bags and wrapping papers were stored and sometimes the thin mewings of tiny wriggling kittens could be heard when the shop cat had given birth on old sacking in a cardboard box.

John was King of the "Dispatch," but sometimes Randall helped with the checking leaving his tiny office with its secure tobacco cupboard beyond. They packed the customers' orders tightly into cardboard boxes and stood them in piles on the floor to await collection by the van drivers for their particular rounds.

Three vans delivered seven hundred orders a week over a wide surrounding area. There was much chat and banter, and remarks about customers that were not always favourable. I asked my grandfather after he had castigated a customer over the phone for some shortcoming. "I thought the customer was always right". "Some customers aren't worth having," he growled.

Two wooden storehouses were erected beyond the dispatch room. Food delivered by suppliers in boxes, chests and sacks were stacked on the rough concreted floors. In the summer jars full of buzzing wasps elbowing their way to the bait of jam at the bottom stood on shelves near the entrance. The dry sickly-sweet odour of mice hung in the far corners despite the strenuous efforts of the shop cats to remove the source of the smell.

Once the family had moved from Rose Cottage into the flat above the new shop, Joan had a room of her own for the first time. The three boys must have shared the end bedroom but Roly was not there for long because he was the first to marry. It was agreed that when Randall married he should live in the flat and John and Emilie would have a house built further down the St Albans Road. So it was in the flat that the young couple crept about in the dark on the night after their wedding.

The flat was approached through a gate at the side of the shop with smooth rounded edged concrete steps to the first floor. Cleaning them was a chore I myself willingly undertook as a child, enjoying splashing a bucket of water down the long flight and sweeping the cascade with a soft broom. A balcony ran the length of the flat separated by plain galvanized rails from the flat roof of the rear part of the shop. At that height one could look across the storehouses and the back lane to a spinney where tall elms, etched against the sky, were studded with the sturdily built nests of a large 'parliament' of rooks. We would watch the birds sitting on nests that swayed precariously in high winds.

The front door was set back into a porch wide and large enough that, after my birth, a wooden gate was slotted in on fine days to make a playpen for me, and later for my brother. The back porch at the far end of the balcony led into the kitchen and opposite to the coal hole. The small kitchen contained a Belfast sink with a wooden draining board, an airing cupboard, table, two chairs, cooking stove and boiler. It was crowded. There was a walk-in larder leading off it in which all the food was stored – jars of jam, bottled fruit; jugs of milk, covered by muslin squares weighted down with glass beads, were placed in bowls of cold water in summer. And when eggs were cheaper they would be preserved in a large stoneware bowl filled with isinglass. That was how the larder looked when I was small. I remember rushing to hide in it when the coalmen came with hefty black sacks over their shoulders to empty coal into the adjoining cupboard. It made a noise that terrified me and I imagined ogres, so I can't think why I wanted to be anywhere near. Mog and Gran did most of the washing by hand using a large saucepan on the gas stove in which to boil whites. Sheets, towels and tablecloths were placed in a grey heavy-duty cardboard box secured with a leather strap and were sent to the laundry in Wellfield Road.

The small dining room was square with the window set at an angle. Three small armchairs with wooden arms, a sideboard, extending table, four dining chairs and a narrow bureau with bookcase sound far too much furniture for the size of the room. The polished wooden mantelpiece held an Art deco Mantel clock and two brass candlesticks. There was no central heating so for much of the year we lived in that room during the week and only lit a fire in the sitting room at the far end of the flat at the weekends or if we had visitors. The stove, where I had my baths, toasted our fronts, but left our backs vulnerable to draughts. It took courage in winter to go to the lavatory or wend one's way to bed. The sitting room had an open fire. The room was less crowded with a three-piece suite, occasional tables and a bookcase. One bedroom had a stove but the other two were inadequately heated by small gas fires. In winter flannels could be frozen by morning and lacy patterns of frost decorated the inside of the windows.

There was a central hall and facing the front door a large oil painting of a country scene at sunset. Beside a calm river walked a woman and a child – though for years I thought it was a motorbike and sidecar.

One of my earliest memories was crawling up the hall pulling a little milk float and carefully placing tiny wooden bottles of milk beside the doors of the two bedrooms on one side, bathroom and separate lavatory on the right. We used to have silly fun over that one lavatory. When someone was inside, two of us would gather umbrellas and walking sticks and prop them quietly against the door so that the occupant would get a surprise when he or she came out. I suspect that when it happened to me it was because I had been inside for a long time. On the door was a large sporting calendar giving fixtures for horse racing, football and cricket and I would lean forward trying to read and memorize the details .

The decorations throughout the flat had been chosen by Grandma Tingey when they moved there in 1933. "Gran Tingey always had a good eye for wall paper," said my mother, and certainly the patterns of flowers and leaves though dark, were unusual and striking. All the wooden doors, windows and skirting boards were distressed and grained in warm toffee coloured varnish in the thirties fashion.

Newtown, itself, had grown since Jonathan Edmund started his business 64 years before. The shops, houses and pubs all showed signs of prosperity. J.E.'s first shop was let by John Tingey to Charlie Moore, a newsagent and tobacconist when the new shop was built, and beside it was the bakery owned by William Hulks. We would go across the road to buy newly baked bread that smelled yeasty and delectable. Otherwise little had changed on the north side of the road. On the south side building had greatly increased. Furthest away from the shop and opposite St Luke's church, there was a Memorial Hall built to commemorate the fallen of the First World War. This was used for social activities, jumble sales and dinners. The "Emporium" of Tingey's Furniture shop, had three large plate glass windows displaying all the latest dining suites and chairs. By this time Tom Tingey had also built a china and ironmongery shop on the other side of French Horn Lane so the top of that road was known as Tingey's Corner. Tom had continued to develop Newtown by building a row of shops for rent. These provided the basic needs of the inhabitants: a fishmonger - Kipper Smith, who played football with Randall - Dollimores, the greengrocer and Butler's, the butcher. Savilles, who had taken over the post office from the Tingeys, moved from the first Right of way to the new row of shops. They also sold stationery and a few books.

An Electricity showroom, wireless shop, two chemists, a men's clothing store and an odd and gloomy haberdashers

St. Albans Road c.1925-30

owned by my great-aunt, May Kentish, almost filled in that side of the road until 101 - Tingeys, the grocers - was reached. There was one open space beside the Electricity showroom which Tom Tingey owned. He had been approached by Sainsburys who wanted to build there. He thought it would harm his brother's trade and declined the offer. It remained a paddock and was used for the horses of Holliers' dairy until the town was developed in 1950.

Inside the flat the dining room window faced west up St Albans road. There, when small, I would look out at the sunset and imagine palaces and cities amongst golden and rosy clouds. The road itself was flanked on the left by the long double row of terrace houses known as Gracemead, built by the Great Northern Railway Company around 1901 for their employees. On the opposite side first came the Robin Hood pub, whose hanging sign squealed and creaked in the wind in the silence of the night, then Rose Cottage and another fine early Victorian house which was the home, when I was a child, of our G.P., Dr. Lamb, and doubled as a surgery. Beyond it there were attractive cottages built of Hertfordshire flint, Streader's saw mill and a blacksmith until the terrace of shops was built in the thirties with the Regent cinema in the middle of them. I only remember one of those: Retty's, where we could buy cornets of delicious ice cream with tiny water crystals in it.

Newtown throughout my childhood was a people-sized place and packed with characters. Everyone knew each other's business; nosey, perhaps, but they cared for one another and news of illness, mishap, or reasons for celebration flew along the road and up and down the Right of Ways. All knew each other's foibles and faults, and by and large accommodated them. Old Miss White in her long black petticoat and black straw hat gave out religious tracts by the One Bell, spent time in the church and stored sandwiches in her voluminous knickers, rooting for them in her pew at lunch time. She was odd but accepted. Clara Viner, who wore voluminous skirts and whose shoes always appeared much too large, was a quiet old lady not asking much of life. She had a penchant for attending funerals and weddings as an onlooker and could be seen at St Luke's waiting for a cortege to arrive. Benny Bishop, with walnut wrinkled face wearing a filthy mackintosh and a droopy tweed hat, was a useful hands-on vet, riding to his customers on a rusty old bike, drooping fag in mouth, his tools of trade in a box on the back.

Some of the inhabitants of the Rights of Way were noisy at night. The exodus from the Boar and Castle opposite our flat was like an episode from *The Waste Land*:

HURRY UP PLEASE ITS TIME
Goo'night Bill. Goo'night Lou. Goo'night May. Goo'night.
Ta ta. Goo'night. Goo'night.[29]

The pub chiefly sold draught beer and it would amuse us to see some nearby residents pop into the Public bar with a jug under their aprons to get a pint. And apocryphal or not, my father recounted a snatch of conversation in the same bar, "Was that you in bed the other side of Lil last night? 'Cos if it was, move over a bit another time. I had no blankets." One old farm labourer having been turned out of the Boar & Castle for being drunk, picked up a brick and threw it meaning to break the pub window, but having accidentally twisted round, he broke one of our shop windows. Up before the magistrate he apologized: "Yer honour I am very sorry. I wouldna broke old John's winder fer anyfink."

Chief among the eccentrics was one of our own family: Auntie May, my grandfather's sister closest to him in age. What made her strange? Everything. I was told that in her youth,

---

[29] T. S. Eliot: Excerpt from The Waste Land 1922. Published in Collected poems. Faber and Faber. 1936

debarred from seeing a dying sister, she climbed up the drainpipe into the bedroom, hoping the sister would remember her in her will or give her some valuable memento. She had married a long-suffering, long-faced man who was a Bank messenger and after marriage they lived in London and had two children there. When they moved back to Hatfield Auntie May had a shop three doors away from ours and the family lived in the flat above. The shop was ostensibly a drapers for women, lined with shelves and glass fronted drawers, but I suspect few people bought anything for it was dirty and unkempt. Besides, once inside people could not get away for Auntie May was a compulsive and frenetic talker. In or out of the shop, her gaunt figure swathed in an ancient cerise coat with a mangy fur collar, and on her head an old purple hat garnished with drooping felt flowers, she would accost almost anyone who passed, grip their arm with bony fingers and tittle-tattle malignant gossip. I was terrified of her. Seeing her coming, people would cross the road quickly and sometimes neighbours would rescue each other by claiming some spurious but urgent excuse for the victim to go home at once. Her daughter Audrey grew up to be very like her in appearance but lacked the panache.

Less fearsome but characterful was old Mrs. Gray, who had piercing dark eyes and lived up one of the Right of Ways. She knew the birthdays of almost everyone in Newtown and much of their history. My mother reckoned that in earlier times she would have been burned as witch. She was kindly, though. I remember one Christmas, when in my teens, Mog and I took her a small present and she insisted on giving us a tumbler each of her blackberry wine. We came away in the dark, stumbling on the rough ground of the narrow lane and holding each other with linked arms for we were very merry.

Also accepted were the Smith family, genuine Romany gypsies, who owned land down Lemsford Road. Their brightly painted caravans were always a source of interest and there were one or two memorable funerals. Local people were respectful at such times and did not attend or go near.

The shop assistants were, of course, local people and several of them loomed large in our family life. By the 1930s Josh Rumney and Mr. Powers were the chief assistants in the grocery department. Mr. Powers was older, small and prim with closely clipped white and a neat moustache carefully twisted at the ends. He was liked by customers for his efficiency and politeness but lacked Josh's bluff friendliness.

Josh, whose proper name was Albert Edward Rumney, had sparse, gingery hair and a toothbrush moustache. He always wore a bow tie and when off duty as a young man might be seen in yellow spats. He saw service as a driver in the Royal Field Artillery in the First World War and then became one of the roundsmen, wearing a heavy mackintosh and brown polished leggings, and eventually became a counter assistant. Sometimes though, customers had to wait while Josh ran to the door of the shop. He had been very fond of his horses when he was in the army and could not hear the clop of hooves without rushing out to see them pass. When my grandmother came to live with us she and Josh would vie with each other to shovel up any horse manure in the road for use in the garden. Mothers would bring small boys to Josh to have "blakeys" (metal tips) on the heels of their boots. He would grab a small leg and hold it between his knees, then hammer home the blakey as if he were shoeing a horse.

When I knew him he was living with his sister, Nellie, in a flint terraced cottage further up the St Albans Road and it was she who laundered the shop assistant's jackets and aprons to stiff, pristine whiteness. She was a kind little woman. Every Christmas from when I was about eight, knowing that I, like her, listened to the Classic serial on my crystal set radio on a Sunday evening, would give me one of the books that had been dramatized. They came in Nelson's blue bound volumes -

Dickens, Harrison Ainsworth, Charles Reade's, *The Cloister and the Hearth*. I was urged to thank her personally and would be given tea in her small parlour seated in a worn armchair, its back adorned with a clean antimacassar, its arms scored by the claws of a much loved tabby cat.

But I am running well ahead of myself. In order of chronology I have not yet been born!

My mother had been visiting Newtown for several years but now she was ensconced in her very own home. The first years of marriage must have been very different for young women when they were no longer expected to have a job and had to depend on their husbands for all their money. But Mog adapted quickly and enjoyed the experience.

> The first two years of our marriage were happy and quiet. I often used to go to Fleetville to see my mum. It was fun going to St Albans on the bus, seeing the "Girls" at Spary and Holiday's. Miss Spary and Miss Holiday had retired and the staff had taken over the shop.

I do not know how far my mother entered into whatever social life there was in the town. Being from "off" she may have taken a little time to work her way in and some of the women would have been a little shy of her. Although most of the tradesmen had grown up in the town and many of the men played football together there was not the same camaraderie among the girls. The Tingeys' grocery, furniture and hardware businesses were by far the biggest shops in Newtown – so the family was a big fish in a small pond. After a while she began to see something of the wives of Randall's football and tennis companions and several of them became her friends at various times through her life. She continued for a while to play netball for a team in St Albans, but she did not play tennis nor did she often go to football matches. As a child I occasionally went with my father when he became a mere spectator. I say "mere" but he was surprisingly vociferous. I was amazed to hear my mild Dad telling the referee "to buy some glasses" or "get on your bike".

Mog did get to know the assistants in the shop. The family business had stability for both employers and employees and made a cohesive little community. She did not work there until staff were called up during World War II but gradually began to be an extra-mural personnel manager, for the 18 - 20 staff. She would visit any who were sick and meet their wives and families. And it really was a family concern at that time for Roly, Randall's next brother, worked there for a while, though he did not settle and later went into farming. Joan began work in the office in 1931. She told me that having had no encouragement to do anything else she had no expectations of a different career. Norman, the youngest son, at sixteen had been sent to train with a wholesale grocer in London. He was given his train fare; ate baked beans on toast every lunch time and heard Oswald Moseley on Tower Hill. But it was not long before he too joined the family business and, being based at the provision counter, became the front of house man. He was more genial than his brother Randall who managed all the finances and was usually to be found in his office.

In December, of course, everyone joined in with the decoration of the windows, the unpacking of special goods and extra deliveries. Christmas was virtually the only time of the year when customers bought food that was richer and different fare from the rest of the year: decorative tins of chocolate biscuits, Turkish delight, puddings, crackers, Stone's ginger wine. crystallised fruits, boxes of dates, muscatel grapes. It was an exciting heady mix, something hard to remember or recreate in these more affluent times.

In 1935 Mog became pregnant. For my 65th birthday she wrote a short essay about my birth:

Randall and I had been married for about eighteen months when we knew a baby was on the way. This was confirmed when visiting Dr. Lamb on the first of three monthly visits. These were stepped up in the last month. I was pleased to buy a ¾ length navy coat and skirt which did not show my condition.

The first thing was to book Nurse Reed who was one of the town's treasures. Mine was to be her 365th baby. Randall and his siblings had also been delivered by her.

To look after mother, baby, plus family, but with no housework would cost 12guineas a month.

Then to assemble all the baby things:
A basket, decorated, to hold pins, powder, soap etc.
A crib draped in muslin
4 vests, 4 flannel gowns
4 nightdresses
4 silk day dresses
Bootees, 6 bibs
1large shawl, 2 small shawls
2 dozen muslin nappies
2 dozen Turkish towelling nappies
A knitted bonnet

The cost of these was about £8.0.0d
Later a high-pram (Cost £7.7.0d)
Mother's needs – apart from nightdresses etc.
Sanitary towels
Mackintosh sheet
Hot water bottle
Soap and talcum powder
Bed pan

Two weeks before Nurse Reed's expected arrival a friend called to ask if the nurse could help them as her mother had had an operation. This was agreed on condition that Nurse came to us when needed.

I was to give birth in the end bedroom which was to be the nursery and the stove there needed attention. The workman took it out, leaving it on the floor. I was visiting a friend with her new baby and she said as I left, "Now, you go home and have yours." My answer was "I can't, the stove is in the middle of the room." But the next morning I woke with a pain. By breakfast time Randall and I were a bit worried, so we sent for Nurse. "Nothing to worry about," she said firmly "It will be a long time yet. I'll come at tea-time".

Of course, I had followed the Motherhood Book which instructed "Carry on as usual. Prepare the bed etc." Nurse Reed arrived with her case at 4 o'clock. At tea-time she looked at me and said "I'll put my uniform on, no need to think of bed." At six o'clock she phoned Dr. Lamb.

"Nurse speaking. Mrs. Tingey's baby is on its way. All's well."

"I had better put off my surgery," replied the doctor and came from his house across the road.

Randall was sent downstairs to occupy himself in the shop. My brother phoned but was told to call later.

We went into the bedroom. I had a bottle of chloroform on the bedpost with a nozzle attached and this I should have been sniffing but more often than not it just banged on my nose. Janet Hope Tingey was born at 7.10pm on October 29th 1935.

All was well. Randall was pleased. He went to see my mother, greeting her with "Good evening, Grandma." My brother, Ben, phoned again and was told "Mother and Baby are asleep. You may come tomorrow."

John Groom, the workman, came in the morning and finished the fireplace.

I was not allowed out of bed for two weeks which meant using the bedpan. After use, Nurse would put a few live coals on a shovel with sprigs of dried lavender and circle the room to make "all things sweet." She was doing this one day when Dr. Lamb walked in, much to her embarrassment.

After a fortnight of pampering I was up and about. Nurse Reed was wonderful, doing all our washing as well as the baby's and cooking for us and any visitors. "How many prunes do you like for breakfast?" she would ask Randall, putting them to soak overnight.

The christening was arranged as Nurse always liked to carry the baby in its christening robes to the church before she left at the month's end.

The Motherhood Book which she mentioned was published by Allied Newspapers and based on the work of Truby King (1858-1938) a New Zealand health reformer. It was a comprehensive book "For the Expectant mother and Baby's First years." It contained everything from precautions during pregnancy, all the preparations, discussion on natural and artificial feeding; feeding timetables – every four hours, no latitude allowed, ignore crying before the time for the feed - baby's weight, baby's daily routine, names, nursery remedies [lots of gripe water] clothing, toys. Mog passed the book on to our daughter Kate in 1970 and her dolls were subjected to its strict regime.

No doubt twenty-five years previously Mog's mother had given birth at home with the help of a neighbour. Perhaps there was an older lady in Arthur Road who, like Ben Hope's mother, Louisa, attended all the pregnancies. Since it was "an easy birth" that would have been deemed sufficient.

Twenty-seven years later I gave birth to our first daughter in Hertford hospital – there being no beds available in the hospital at Stevenage where we lived. I wanted to have my baby at home but my father in law who was a doctor, was worried at the idea and so – having drawn out my teacher's three-year old pension contributions to pay for it – I spent ten days in idleness, seeing Kate for feeds, reading magazines and Jane Austen. But the birth was so easy that three years later I insisted on having the next baby at home. No living in nurse for us. It was intended that my mother would come but she was taken ill so we managed. With signs of the baby being urgently on its way we phoned Mrs. Draper, the midwife in the morning and she and Miss Rose, a trainee from Jamaica, came to ensure all was ready. They said they would return after the doctor's clinic unless I rang.

Three-year old Kate came home after a happy morning at a friend's house and wanted to tell me all about it while bouncing on my distended stomach. I persuaded her to have lunch. Mark came home at three o'clock, played with Kate and we decided he should take her for a walk. Neither of us felt it was obligatory for him to be there at the moment of birth. Mrs. Draper came, examined me and said it would not be long. She went off to see another case and her assistant begged that if I could wait until her clean smock was brought back, she would be grateful, so wait we did. As soon as both smock and the midwife returned, I went on the bed and half-hour later Nell was born.

Father and sister came in to see her and Kate, with wonder in her face, expressed profound satisfaction that she had a sister.

Maybe I am wrong – and after all we three women, Annie, Mog and I had easy uncomplicated deliveries – but fifty years later giving birth seems, as an onlooker, to be hedged about with health and safety, medicine and technology. This could be awesome for some young mothers, so that some of the straightforwardness and simplicity is lost.

My mother found that my birth in 1935 added a lot to her life and brought her friends and relations to Hatfield. She said:

> I was very proud of my baby and my high pram. I used to walk the four miles to Fleetville and spend the day with Mother. Randall used to come by van after the shop had shut to take us both home. We often went to Grandma Tingey's too. Janet was not her first grandchild for Roly already had a daughter, but she was welcoming and we used to sit in the garden gently rocking the pram to send Janet to sleep.

Both my parents had some talent for drawing and they decorated the "nursery" with pen and ink sketches of teddy bears, characters from Beatrix Potter, dolls and golliwogs, mostly copied but some original, glued to a long strip of paper and made into a frieze.

So I entered this story and became another leaf on the family tree.

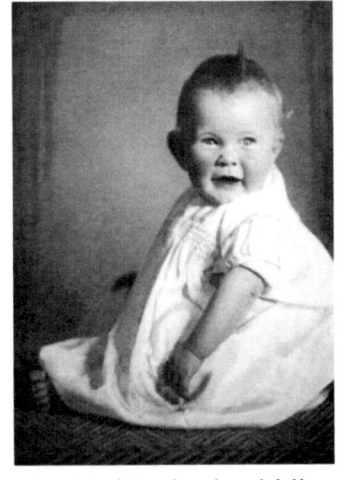

Mog began to interest herself in the garden which was at the side of the shop. An orchard behind it had been part of the allotments on which the new shop had been built. The front which bordered the road was set with shrubs, hiding the garden from passers-by. There was a lawn of sorts, then some fussy arbours where, before my second birthday, my mother had dug a square hole and made me a sandpit. There was a trellis with climbing roses, a shed and beyond an area of kitchen garden. And at the back a simple picket fence with a hawthorn hedge in front separated the garden from an unmade lane, known as the Back Way. This ran from French Horn Lane to Dog Kennel Lane[30]. In earlier days Mr. Hill of Roe Green Farm having had sheep unloaded from the railway station drove them early in the morning down the Back way and over the fields to his farm.

Mog wrote no more about the early days of her marriage. There must have been adjustments between the couple as there are in any marriage. My father was not always easy. He hated parties so that excuses were often made and Mog silently repined. Indeed, in old age he said he would only go to houses where he could wear his slippers, but he enjoyed the company of his good neighbours and longstanding friends. Mog would have loved to go dancing. Maypole dancing at school, Scottish dancing in St Albans with a friend had been fun but once she was married all this stopped. My father had never learned to dance and could not have been persuaded. Though he had been a member of the Hatfield Pirates he had avoided the social events. His cousin Eric said that every Saturday night they had a dance and a teacher came over from St Albans to teach them to dance properly and girls came but not Randall. There was also a theatrical company but Randall did not join.

Years later when my brother was a teenager my mother and her friends were determined that their children should learn to dance. One winter Bill and his cousin Richard would be driven reluctantly over to Welwyn Garden City along with two girls, the daughters of a neighbour, to learn ballroom dancing for it was just before the days of rock'n roll. The boys would be cajoled, forced, into wearing suits and attending the end of the term dance. Asked if he had enjoyed it on his return, Bill grunted. "Which dances did you do?" pressed Mog. "Well, we

---

[30] Named from the 18th century when the 1st Marchioness of Salisbury, an avid huntswoman, kept her pack of hounds there

did learn a new one called 'Strip the Widow'" he replied without enthusiasm.

So Randall, as a young married man, was shy and retiring and could be uncommunicative at home. I don't know when, but there was a time when he would be virtually silent for days and my mother would sit in the lavatory and cry. But don't misunderstand me: it was a very happy marriage. I suspect that Mog made more adjustments than he for it was the first half of the twentieth century and perhaps it was so with many women. Marriage gradually gave Randall more confidence so that he showed a genuine and cheerful interest in one's doings. He was an enthusiastic playmate and companion in my childhood. And when relaxed amongst the family he showed a sense of fun and wit that was delightful. He was also a good shopkeeper for over forty years - caring for both employee and customer. In a letter written after his death, his daughter in law said:

> Pop was more than anyone could wish for as a father in law - more like my own father and friend combined. He was loving, kind and infuriatingly stubborn at times.

It was a stubbornness and independence that rounded out his character. It was hard to persuade him to go on holiday for he disliked new places. Yet if persuaded then it was easy to get him to return.

But all this was to come. Before the start of World War II there was time for relaxation. At home, Mog enjoyed her cooking and needlework. She made all my dresses, smocking them with increasing skill, and continued to make all her own clothes. Pop would read, mostly non-fiction, listen and fiddle with his short-wave radio. He thought he would make a model of an aeroplane from a kit one winter but became quickly impatient with his clumsiness and he threw it into the fire. He told me that with his first wages from the shop he had bought a second-hand violin but when he found that squeaks were all he could achieve he quickly sold it to a friend. My tendency to give up must be inherited from him. As W.C. Fields said, "If at first you don't succeed, try, try again. Then quit. There's no point in being a damn fool about it." It could be our motto.

How soon my own memories come into this story is uncertain. Perhaps I only remember what I have been told. My mother experienced the usual sorts of mishaps with me. There was the day she looked into the cot in the twilight of evening. I was asleep but looked so pale and ill that she panicked momentarily until she saw an open jar of zinc and castor oil amongst the blankets. She had left it without its lid having greased my bottom and I had smeared it generously over my face.

It equates with the occasion when my Kate found a jar of Avon face cream, polished the coffee table with it so that the sitting room smelled like a high-class brothel. Or worse, there was the evening when having prepared a Yorkshire pudding mixture and left it in the fridge, I picked it up, instead of the Cow and Gate milk, and fed it to my six week old daughter. Couldn't understand why the teat kept blocking up. I was so ashamed I did not tell anyone about the mishap for years.

Apart from going over to Fleetville to visit Gran Hope, I have few genuine memories of the period just before the war. Maybe, though, it was then that my mother took me to see Miss Spary and Miss Holliday. The sitting room in their house in St Albans that Mog and her friend, Nell, had found for them, was furnished with antiques and there were cabinets displaying china figurines. The glow from the open fire twinkled on the gold rims of their tea set. And tea consisted of tiny cucumber sandwiches, Victoria sponge and macaroons. Miss Holliday was wore a lace fichu over her dove grey dress and she smelled of lavender while Miss Spary was brisk and mannish. I was allowed to play with a Victorian paperweight. When I turned it upside down thick snow fell upon a tiny village scene. It was enchanting and I coveted it. Sadly they did not give it to me as Miss Ure had done with her tea set.

My mother's quiet domestic life with her baby; the cosy afternoon tea served by Miss Spary's maid in their peaceful sitting room, the luxury Christmas groceries, all might serve as postscripts to the Thirties. It seems now a cosy, somewhat naïve world; dim, fragmented memories for me but they must have been clear in the mind of my mother when she looked back on them in the harsh, grey days of war.

Undoubtedly my parents, like many others in the country, had no stomach for another World War only twenty years after the first. Then Mog had lost her father; two of Randall's uncles had died and his parents were afflicted by the tragedies of the Randall family. Although with hindsight we can see that Churchill was right to try to wake up government and country to the dominance and aggression of Hitler, nonetheless we can understand the desires of most of the British population that welcomed Chamberlain's efforts to secure peace. I remember, as a teenager, being somewhat ashamed when I saw the letter which my parents received from 10 Downing Street in 1938, thanking them for their appreciation of his efforts to secure a non-aggression pact with Hitler at Munich; coming back hopefully declaring that he had brought back "Peace for our time". Did he believe it? Did they? Was he just trying to gain time? I cannot speak for Chamberlain but I suspect that Mog and Pop were realistic enough to know that it was unlikely but felt they wanted to support someone who had done his best.

In the summer of 1940 my mother made a scrapbook for her friend Nell's birthday, for Nell was my godmother. That too is perhaps a piece of nostalgia. It is postcard size and consists of snapshots of me from the age of three months to four years. I am in my pram, solemnly hugging my woolly dog, while waiting to be taken for a walk; toddling at 11½ months; aged 18 months pushing my horse on wheels towards my smiling father; standing beside him on the beach as he pointed out to sea. We had been to Rustington in Sussex for a holiday in the summer of 1938; a week of which I remember little other than the horrible discomfort of my hand-knitted raspberry coloured bathing costume which sagged unbecomingly around my knees as I came out of the water. Each photo has a caption written by Mog: "I'm ready!", "Playmates", "Westward Ho!" But the last two look forward. There I am, standing to attention with my Uncle Norman who is in uniform and the last photo shows me mounted on Ben, my toy horse, holding a toasting fork on my shoulder and with a tea cosy on my head. "Britain's Secret Weapon." Is the caption underneath.

Chapter 6

Chasing Hitler on a dining room chair.

Cries and fierce growls terrified me. Certain that there was a large grey wolf in the sitting room next door, I threw on my red dressing gown, ran out of the bedroom and unbolted the front door. I rushed down the stairs and out to the front gate. Suddenly the scenario changed. There was Adolph Hitler, black cropped hair, neat moustache and uniform immediately recognizable, speeding past the gate in a red sports car. In a second I was in hot pursuit careering up St Albans Road on one of our dining room chairs. Before reaching the cinema I would wake disturbed and breathless. Not the only mad dream I have had in my life but certainly the one that recurred most often, probably for about four or five years and it began early in the Second World War. The war essentially framed my early years and although I do not remember being consciously frightened until doodlebugs invaded the air in 1944 my subconscious mind was obviously affected much earlier.

****

My fluffy pram blanket, wrapped firmly around me, tickled my nose. I was being carried down the steps from the flat on a cold winter's night. Stars blazed in a coal black sky. It is my most vivid snapshot of the early days of the war. We were going down to our air raid shelter which was in the garden at the back of the shop. We called it the Dugout – because it had been dug out of the orchard at the back of the shop. My father had been ordered to have it built in 1938 when rumours of war were multiplying. Half below ground level, the top was covered by earth and turfs and it was large enough to hold a shopful of customers if there was air raid during the day. The entrance had a narrow door and an escape exit at the far end. The walls were of ridged concrete and were clammy with damp, even oozing with water at times. Wooden benches ran up each side for seating with duck boards on the ground. After the war the shelter became an admirable cheese store, being dark, cool but far from dry; after heavy rain the duckboards on the floor floated. Food safety officials would not regard it kindly today.

Around 11am on the first day of the war (a Sunday), when several of the shop staff were filling shelves, an alert sounded and in no time everyone disappeared not to the dugout but to their homes. In the early days staff and customers did use it in the daytime although they mostly stood about outside. The shops closed at dusk or earlier so then it was only used by us.

The dugout was not the only preparation that was made in advance of the outbreak of war. Also in 1938 gas masks were issued. My mother volunteered to go to the public hall to assemble them. The metal piece was affixed to the rest by a strong rubber band. She said you could spot all those who had worked on them because they all had plasters on their fingers which had been rubbed raw. Mog's private preparation in 1940 was to make me memorise my National Identity card number: DFEN1743. She also persuaded me to don my gas mask while doing a little dusting round the house so I got used to the damp stickiness and the rubbery smell. I don't know why I was not issued with a Mickey Mouse mask. I was young enough. Perhaps there were not enough to go round. Mog assuaged my disappointment by saying it made me very grown up.

In the spring of 1939 Hatfield Council had been told that they would be allocated 3600 evacuees and the weekend before the outbreak of war the first contingent arrived, being brought in London Transport buses from North London to the North front of Hatfield House.

We had two girls billeted with us but the experience was not happy and positive like that of the Hopes with Hodge

Uphill. Barbara and Jinnie were around ten and twelve, I believe. I suppose that my parents and Gran Hope had never come across London kids from a poor home before. I know that my mother, usually open minded, found their table manners crude and their speech difficult to understand. When they commented that their bedroom smelt of apples she did not tell them that the season's Bramleys were stored on top of the wardrobe for she feared they would have a midnight feast. At four years old, I just watched them with wonderment. Poor kids. They must have felt so homesick and totally out of their element. They came with few clothes in a battered suitcase but Mog acquired more and bought new shoes for them. By the beginning of January she mentioned in her diary that she had helped them with their homework but she was beginning to take a bigger part in the running of the shop and decided that the girls should move elsewhere. She refused the first offer of a new billet on the 13th January, saying tersely in her pocket diary "Rotten woman" but found another more congenial in February. Very soon, however, like many others, the girls returned to London.

There was another wave of evacuation in the early autumn of 1940 following the German invasion of France and the beginning of the Blitz. My mother, as part of her Red Cross duties, sat at a desk in the primary school at Dellfield and waited for the children to arrive. There must have been an air raid warning for suddenly the billeting officer dashed into the room shouting "They're here, they're here!" Ever efficient, my mother said "Well, please get them to line up and come in one by one." "Not them, you bloody fool, the Jerries!"

Throughout the Blitz from September 1940 to the summer of 1941 we spent every night in the dugout. I had a mattress with sheets and blankets on the bench and for my headboard the linen chest from our bathroom filled with a set of Harmsworth's Encyclopaedias to keep it in place. Towards the end of the war when we were again sojourning in the shelter for fear of V2s, I would take out a volume from the chest and study its black and white pictures. I never imagined that one day I might actually visit Machu Picchu or Samarkand. Then such exotic places might have been on the moon.

My parents and Gran Hope slept, fully dressed and swaddled in blankets, in deckchairs with foot rests, which could hardly have given them sufficient rest. A neighbour, Nancy Bennett, slept in another deckchair next to Gran Hope. Her brother was an air raid warden and she did not like to be alone. One night there was a commotion at the back of the shelter and my parents woke in consternation. Was it an invasion? No, it was Nancy B who, caught short, had tried to climb out of the emergency exit at the back of the shelter. Another time, when dreaming she burst forth in song "South of the Border down Mexico way" – an incident with which she was teased for a long time.

One night early in the war there was a commotion outside. Voices raised and footsteps on the roof above. Was it parachutists? The invasion? It woke us all in a fright. Then a peremptory knock on the door, "Is Mr. Tingey there?" My father hesitantly went outside. Near the Dugout was a large square pit in which rubbish from the shop was burned. No rubbish collection in those days, no recycling. Cardboard, wood, broken eggs, rotten oranges were all burned there giving off acrid smells. The fire was usually damped down and carefully extinguished by nightfall but on this occasion something had ignited and blazed forth. The police had sent for the fire brigade and it was the firemen who had clambered on the roof to hose down the flames. I suspect that we were given a warning for possibly helping German planes to find their way to the de Havilland's aerodrome but I don't think we were fined and it never happened again.

Was it necessary to spend all those nights of discomfort in the dugout? I suppose it was easier to settle down at night in a safe place rather than be disturbed by the siren in the middle of the night. I once asked my mother if she and my father ever stayed upstairs so they could make love. They were, after all only thirty at the beginning of the war. Mog giggled with embarrassment. "We did not like to go up to the flat. It was too far if there was an air raid, so just occasionally we used to take rugs and pillows and put them on the sacks in the warehouse."

Do I remember the thin, austere voice of Neville Chamberlain in September 1939 saying: "…and consequently this country is at war with Germany"? I think I do. We were all sitting round the large Murphy wireless in the dining room at the flat, and I sensed the seriousness and black depression of the adults. Throughout the war the wireless was the focus of so many broadcasts. With its polished maple wood case and tweedy cloth covering the speaker, it dominated the wall beside my father's armchair. Occasionally it would be Lord Haw Haw's voice that brought gloom to the dining room or reports from German radio. Above it hung a large shiny map of the world in which my dad would insert pins denoting battles and reverses.

My father kept a diary for much of his life. Often they were Letts page a day volumes so that he could write quite extensively in his flowing, legible handwriting. And that was an achievement for when he started school and was found to be naturally left-handed he was made to write with his other hand. Not all the books have survived but I have browsed those that did and his words have helped my remembrances. Mog's diaries were more to do with household expenditure with some additions. Her tiny diary for 1940 – about 6x10cm – contains, for a few weeks, notes on her activities and the weather and gives a brief description of that first cold winter of the war[31]:

January
15th Getting colder. Had to dry washing in the sitting room.
19th All frozen up. Just one tap running.
20th Coldest day for 59 years.
21st Black Sunday.
23rd Made snowman with Jan.
24th Thawed!!! Thank God. Soldiers had soup.
25th Bought snow shoes.
28th Snowed, snowed and snowed. 12 inches on the flat roof.
29th Washing froze on line.
31st Jan helped me scrape paths in the snow with coal shovels.

She recorded little after that other than her shifts for the Red Cross, and nothing about the harsh winters in the first three years of the war.

Being seventeen miles from London we did not experience the agonies of the blitz though I did stand one night beside my mother gazing at the lurid glow extending across the sky to the south and wondered why she was in tears.

---

[31] In the '39/'40 winter, not only was snow a significant problem, but it contained the longest-lasting RAIN-ICE event (27th January to 3rd February, 1940) known for these islands, with severe transport dislocation, and many injuries on the ice in a large area from north Wales across parts of the south-west Midlands to the southwest and central-southern England. During the same period, a great snow storm with a violent gale affected southeastern England with snow drifts well above 15 ft. January, 1940. It was the coldest (to that date) of the century, only later beaten by January 1963. No wonder we all had chilblains.

Nonetheless there were incidents of bombing not far away and then on the morning of 3rd October 1940 a Junkers 88 dropped its bombs on de Havilland's aircraft factory and Hatfield knew the war had really arrived. The damage was severe; twenty-one workers lost their lives, and there were many casualties.

I hardly understood the sadness and gloom around the town but the excitement of seeing the smashed and splintered glass covering the pavement where three of the shop's large plate glass windows had broken and fallen is still with me. When most of it had been picked up I was allowed to help, sweeping up the smaller shards of glass with my own dustpan and brush.

It was then that Mog said to Randall: "I think we ought to burn all our love letters. If we get bombed I don't want them to be scattered all over the road for anyone to read". I doubt if the letters were long; I doubt they were explicit or even wildly romantic. Letters had been written when Randall was in hospital in London when he was eighteen, notes were sent between St Albans and Hatfield when they were unable to meet. That evening they opened the closed stove in the dining room and burnt the papers one by one, lingering over a few that held happy memories.

I do not remember when Gran Hope came to live with us. She moved into the second bedroom of the flat, bringing her dressing table with its three fold mirror, a small arm chair, her favourite books and personal possessions. Soon the room acquired comforting smells of wool and lavender. She quickly slotted into the household routines. My mother became heavily involved with the shop and, besides being its unofficial personnel manager, she stepped in when office staff were called up. Though completely unversed in book keeping, and with the help of sixteen year old Pam Cordwell, she took over the office and managed it efficiently. Consequently it was Gran who was at home when I returned from school.

On two nights a week at least and sometimes for a five hour shift Mog, smart in her Red Cross uniform, would go down to Wellfield, once the local workhouse but now housing bedridden old people who had been evacuated from London. At first she would go from 2pm until 7pm and she would often bath "three old dames". Later she changed her shifts to fit in with her work in the office at the shop and in the evenings she was often there alone. She would come home tired but full of stories. She was amused to find that the local doctor placed bets for the old ladies. One patient, just before she was tucked up, would stand precariously on her bed and pull an imaginary chain to extinguish the gaslight. Another who had a bolster down the length of her broken leg to keep it straight would whip it out and whack the nurse if she did not like her treatment. One night the old soul was uncharacteristically quiet when Mog went into the ward. Eventually matron arrived and enquired. "Is she all right?" Mog replied, "Yes, perfectly all right. She is dead".

The Red Cross often involved me for Mog held classes in our sitting room to teach bandaging to new recruits. I sat on the settee, my arms and legs wound in crepe bandages, or one arm put into a sling, learning that the triangular bandage should be tied with a reef knot on the injured side so that it did not pull on the other shoulder. Mog used also to collect for the Red Cross. No standing politely outside a supermarket, carefully avoiding eye contact in those days. My mother would dress me up in a miniature nurse's uniform, give me the tray of flags and off we would go to houses on her beat. Who could resist giving to a six year old nurse?

Mog had belonged to the Red Cross before war started – some compensation for her desire to be a nurse. She was enthusiastic and competent but never good at examinations being nervous of her spelling. The question papers often described a situation and asked the examinee what action she should take. "A gunner…" began one such question and described his wound which was of course, consequent on his occupation, but all my mother could think in panic was "Fancy them giving his name with initials." Nonetheless she became a corporal which was more than my reluctant father achieved in the Home Guard. I was far more warlike than he. To protect our home I would do sentry duty on the front porch in my tin hat. Remember the picture of me standing at attention with my Uncle in uniform? When my father, once only, was issued with a rifle, he reported in his diary:

> We were allowed to take it home but without ammunition. Janet spent the whole evening with its barrel resting on a dining room chair, kneeling down and

squinting along the sights. Then she polished the butt. She was most impressed and excited by it.

I was excited by the oily smell of the metal and the gleaming wooden butt. And of course I could see the enemy skulking amongst bushes within rifle range.

Another part of my "war work" was organised by the wife of the chemist next door to us. She was a contralto of operatic proportions – and pretensions, and was billed as Madame Eluned MacSweeney when she took part in charity concerts She was also a lady with prim ways, insisting that her little daughter, Maureen, wore white gloves and a hat when out, and she always produced, dainty embroidered serviettes when I went round for tea. This was something we did not run to except on festive occasions. She would take Maureen and me down to the convalescent home, Bush Hall, when she entertained the solders. They sat politely in rows, wearing their cornflower blue jackets, white shirts and red ties and she would sing an aria or two and then the poor fellows were subjected to Maureen reciting nursery rhymes – for she was four years younger than I – followed by my spirited rendering of poems:

"Over the river and down the lea,
That's the way for Billy and me!

By the winter of 1945 my performances had grown more sophisticated. This time it was at the old people's home. My father reported:

Jan went to Wellfield to a party at which she is to sing two carols and recite two poems, one of which is The Lion had a Tail. To express this she has taken a bulrush for a tail.

To return to the real war work: my father was sent call up papers in 1941. A shy and pacific man, he would not have been keen to go into the army, but his main concern was the business. His brother Norman was a Territorial and had left for the Royal Artillery in August 1939[32], and as soon as war was declared the immediate impact for the business was the sudden call up of thirteen male assistants and later of four female staff. This was crippling. The grocery business of those days was extremely labour intensive and some of it was skilled work. No plastic wrapped pre-cut rashers of bacon then! Sides of bacon were marched into the yard upon the shoulders of Peter Keevil's delivery men, who wore white hoods with capes to protect them from the salty grease. Then the bacon had to be deftly boned out so as to avoid waste. Sugar arrived in sacks and was packaged neatly in blue bags, the corners folded and tucked under the flap. Tea, which arrived in large plywood chests with protective metal edges and lined with silver paper, was weighed into quarter pounds and poured into decorative bags. Cheeses needed skinning - a difficult job which skinned one's knuckles and broke one's nails; fruit still had to be cleaned, 56lb blocks of butter cut and weighed into ¼ and ½lb packs and wrapped in Tingey's own labelled papers. Dried fruit, arriving in flat wooden boxes had the lids prized up with a jemmy[33] and the fruit scooped and eased out. Gritty and sticky, as in my father's youth, it had to be washed and dried before packing into strong blue bags. Ground almonds, loose and greasy, had to be poured into homemade cones of greaseproof paper.

    Suddenly the skilled men were swept away into the forces. Randall and his father had to find and train female

---

[32] Incidentally taking his father's Studebaker car with him as part of the war machine. He was with the British Expeditionary Force landing at Le Havre and making way towards Paris but they had to retreat when the Germans broke through.

[33] A short crowbar

assistants. My father decided to ask for deferment on the grounds that the business, besides having 3500 registered customers, supplied several hospitals, canteens and children's homes. It also held essential rations of syrup, sugar, bacon and other goods for the local population in the event of an emergency. He added:

> My father is still engaged in the business but at the age of 63 can hardly be expected to take over the entire management, not having taken any part in the buying and accountancy work for ten years, and apart from this the numerous details connected with Food Control which would confuse anyone not having experience of them from the beginning. Apart from the general office work, staff management and buying which keep me busy for twelve hours a day, there are two branch shops which require supervision and at times, owing to the shortage of male assistants I find it necessary to deliver goods myself. While the whole family was employed in running the business each took a share of the responsibility but you will realise that without them the difficulties increase enormously and should I be called up there seems almost certain that the business would have to close.

He was granted deferment for three months and was told to advertise for an older man to replace him. Only one applicant came forward and he had no experience. Deferment was again requested. This became a running saga which was not finally resolved until July 1944.

There was always the possibility that more staff would be called up and one can sense the irritation and weariness in my father's diary:

> March 10, 1943: have spent most of the day completing

the "Manpower" forms which require names and ages of all the staff. This is to see how many we can do without so that some can be sent to more important work. Of course that has a different meaning to the Ministry of Labour than to us. Whoever has to go will probably be sent to a nurses' home to wash up or to a factory to make face cream which is apparently considered essential. It's time the mask was lifted on many things that are done under the cloak of "essential". When you know that men can spend an hour or more in an aircraft works making rings out of threepenny bits it makes you think. And when you've thought what can you do about it?

Randall did join Dad's army. He spent three nights a week at the Home Guard office from 8-10pm booking in and out supplies. He was not an enthusiastic soldier:

1943 January 4th: An unpleasant surprise awaited us at H.G. last night. We were informed that we had to be prepared to pass a test in Rifle shooting, Field craft, First Aid, Gas and General Knowledge. Not having had any experience or training apart from a scattered half hour or so six months ago, and not having handled a rifle since, we were disgusted. This will mean drills and extra duty for a time. I very much dislike anything to do with rifles, First Aid and Gas. As for General Knowledge, whatever that means, I guess there will be some damn silly questions.

One morning at breakfast after being on duty all night he told us that as daylight was breaking he and his companions heard a thunder of noise outside. Quickly jumping to their feet and thinking that perhaps parachutists had been dropped they raced out.

The noise came nearer and then from under the Park viaduct galloped about six horses along the street. We spread ourselves out all three of us and with arms waving, we managed to turn the enemy and chase them back to their field in Park meadow.

Later that week they had a bayonet fighting lesson which he found:

A very crude idea. What with "war-cries" and the language used for commands it was as if we were in the nineteenth century learning to fight redskins.

However, when he marched with his company to the miniature rifle range he was "rather pleased" when he hit the target with all of his five rounds, never having fired a rifle before. And he recorded that he had made a "good attempt" at assembling a Lewis gun. This surprised him for he had "little interest in mechanics".

He did not tell me about such exploits so I remember little of his soldiering other than walking beside him when he was on his way to a parade. I felt proud and, like my mother twenty years before, noticed the salty raw smell of his khaki uniform.

I accompanied my dad when he took large billy cans of hambone and pea soup for the men of the anti-aircraft battery perched on top of a hill near Roe Green. One evening when frost and snow sparkled in the moonlight we transported the can on my homemade wooden sledge and I sat on it for the return journey. I remember very little about our arrival at the camp; just warm thanks and a confusion of voices. The soup may have been hot but Mog's recipe for it does not sound appetizing: Soldiers' Soup (per 4 portions) 6 pints water, 3 large bones, 2 potatoes. 2 onions, 2 large carrots and ½lb split peas, salt and pepper.

Some of the soldiers from the anti-aircraft battery and also some RAF men from de Havillands came to the flat occasionally for tea and a bath in the regulation five inches of water. We welcomed Mrs. Blair who came down from Scotland to be with her husband, Jimmy, when he had a short leave. All this added to our social life. The men played Happy Families and Tiddlywinks with me while no doubt wistfully thinking of their own small children. A long letter from Cpl. John Beattie RAF written from France in July1944 to my father commented that it "is now gone four years since I was fortunate enough to find your friendship". He sent a message to me saying that he hoped I would "come up to Scotland for a holiday as soon as they are settled down again". Sadly that never happened.

Having such visitors, sleeping in the dugout, the bombs, and the regular short absences of my parents was normal life for me, wartime conditions were just part of the weave. As you will have noticed strict chronology has not been making sense for some time. Most things that happened are being seen from my view – knee or waist high – and the incidents float randomly into my memory.

Chapter 7

Battling on

"Is that all?" enquired Mrs. – disbelievingly as Fred Reeves carefully cut and weighed out 4oz [112g] cheese and wrapped it neatly in greaseproof paper.

"Well, Mrs. -, there's only the two of you and that's the ration for the week".

"Mr. – could take all that for 'is bit o' lunch" said Mrs. – indignantly.

"Well, Mrs. – said Fred lamely, "There is a war on."

There were many such conversations when rationing started. When people, some grudgingly, some cheerfully, had become used to the basic rationing there were more questions when points were introduced in 1943. Points allowed a little more choice but items were often not available in sufficient quantity to give every customer what they wanted. When canned fruit was released on points in the spring of 1943 it caused a commotion.

"I think you've got some canned fruit. That'll be a treat. I'll have a tin of apricots".

"Oh, I'm sorry, Mrs.-" replied Mr. Powers, twirling one end of his little white moustache in agitation. "The apricots have all gone. I've got a nice tin of prunes".

"But we don't like prunes. Regular enough without them, thank you very much."

On January 8th 1940 bacon, butter and sugar were rationed by weight and this was followed two months later by meat (by price) and in the summer, cooking fat, tea, jam, biscuits, cereals and cheese. Eggs and milk were rationed by allocating supplies in shops according to the number of their registered customers. The amounts varied considerably over the course of the war.

The whole bureaucracy of rationing imposed a great burden on shop keepers. Customers had to register at their preferred shop and my parents spent many weary hours filling in details because many customers, either through laziness or illiteracy, merely filled in their names and left the shop to put in the addresses.

There were occasional glitches which made record keeping difficult. In October, 1943 the Ministry of Food announced that customers could take sugar in place of jam or vice-versa and were asked to take eight weeks' sugar ration and preserves all at once. My father wondered if this was a forerunner of some reductions or "perhaps a military move – anticipating the need to reduce civilian transport." Sadly it was realized too that some people were receiving more than their share of certain goods by means of tips and bribes and warnings had to be put up in the shop pointing out the consequences. As always, some people were understanding and did not complain but others:

> September 1943: For the second time within a week one of our dear customers has been to the Food office to enquire why she has had no eggs for six weeks (or was it years?) The office phoned me to say in effect that we should have had some since August. In fact that was the last delivery we had.

When clothing points were issued the women assistants in the shop became exasperated with Josh and Mr. Powers who smugly announced that they had plenty of points to spare but never considered passing some to their colleagues to buy stockings or knickers.

The privations of rationing hardly impinged on me. My father and grandfather did not allow the family to have more than their rations from the shop but by the time I was eating family meals it was the status quo. Like many other households we kept chickens and ducks. That the eggs were important can be gathered from the fact that each entry in my dad's diary would be prefaced with the number laid. One egg per person a week as was the ration in towns for much of the war must have been privation. I read recently about of a family in Birmingham in 1943. They had enough to eat but no Christmas fare:

> No chance of turkey or chicken – not even the despised rabbit. If we can get a little mutton that is the best we can hope for...Have managed a Christmas pudding but there are shops with three Christmas puddings and 800 registered customers.[34]

When I was old enough to drink tea my mother gave me it without sugar in order to save the ration. On a visit to old Mrs. Hemmings in the Vineyard cottage in Hatfield Park for tea one summer afternoon I learned how horrid sweetened tea was. Thinking she was giving me a treat, and before Mog could say anything, Mrs. Hemmings stirred two large teaspoons of sugar into my small cup. My mother with a glance warned me to say nothing. I sat on the horsehair filled sofa, its hot leather cover sticking to my thighs and slowly sipped the tea. My mother, making conversation to distract attention from my gloomy face, asked Mrs. Hemmings about the chicken wire gate that was slotted into the door frame. "I suppose that is to keep out the rabbits", she asked. "No, the rats" replied the old lady.

Food was ample but not exciting. For most of my generation the memories are of cabbage, small amounts of meat, corned beef fritters, unrecognizable fish, puddings like

---

[34] Few Eggs and No oranges by Vere Hodgson: Persephone Books 2010

suet 'Sultana roll' boiled in a cloth. Unlike my dad who was addicted to it, I hated custard so my puddings were always somewhat dry. Mog used to make what she called "swimmers" – a term from East Anglia not Hertfordshire. Could it possibly have come down through the family from her butler grandfather? Swimmers were balls of suet or bread dough simmered in water and served as a pudding with golden syrup. There was tinned fruit in varying amounts and we, of course, used any damaged tins and those which had lost their labels. It was disappointing when pudding turned out to be not plums but carrots.

Sometimes small quantities of what had become "luxury" goods came in and it was impossible to distribute these fairly. Those customers who did not tell their neighbours about them were favoured. Strange anomalies could crop up. Early in the war there was a consignment of army hard tack- rock hard, like thick dog biscuits. When one tin was opened there was an array of Huntley and Palmers fancy cheese biscuits, each one tastefully framed in red crinkly paper - cheese straws, tiny pastries, crackers and wafery footballs stuffed with cream cheese. My mother took me down to the office to see them. Alas, when we ventured to try them the biscuits were soft and the cheese rancid.

One day, towards the end of 1944, I was playing in the orchard when my mother came carrying a banana. She showed me how to peel it and was clearly excited and pleased that she could give me one. "Now, you mustn't tell anyone about it", she said, "because we only received one box and we can give one each to customers who will keep quiet about it" The fruit was such a rarity that one of my six year old birthday cards featured a tidy little boy in collar and tie devouring one. I did not like the taste or the texture and Mog was disappointed. I was more enthusiastic when I was given the very occasional orange.

In 1944 my father recorded that he was very low in saleable lines and for one week was "completely out of bacon" which upset people. Sometimes, especially in the months before D-day when movement on roads and railways was almost solely for the military, supplies took so long to get to Hatfield that they had suffered in transit:

13th April, 1944 Of rationed goods we hold a fairly heavy stock: about 4 tons of jams, 2 tons of margarine, 1 ton of lard, 2 tons of cheese, 1 ton of tea. I hope we don't get a price reduction. Spent an hour with Dad sorting oranges. We found about 56lbs were bad and unsaleable. Luckily, although they were part of the consignment in which bombs were found, there were none in our six cases.
[Were there really bombs in the orange boxes?]

My main memory of rationing was the counting of coupons. Having cut the necessary number of points and coupons from the customers' ration books the assistants would put them safely in tins behind the counter. When they were totted up the totals were taken with the bags of coupons to the local Food Office. Once I was old enough it fell often to the lot of my grandmother and me to count the fiddly squares of paper which would blow off the dining room table in the draught of an opening door. We had to put them in piles of a hundred and secure them in bags. Several times when my father had taken them to the Food office an officious clerk would tell him the figures were incorrect. Grumbling but dutiful we re-counted them. On one occasion they were sent back a second time but got the reply that they were not going to be counted again. The figures would have to do. They were. My mother had the idea that the Food Office should keep the coupons to be used as confetti after the war – a novel method of re-cycling. Why not shower them on customers?

Our own diet was supplemented as was that of other people in the country by the gift of an occasional rabbit. Rabbit stew bulked out with suet dumplings was a feast. The rabbits came via the keepers in Hatfield Park and arrived unskinned. Mog would take the opportunity to give me a biology lesson. Seated on a stool by the kitchen table I would watch as she slit open the belly and pointed out the heart and liver. Her attempts at biology did not always work so well. When I asked what our lungs were like she said they were like sponges and for some time I suffered under the delusion of having a Victoria sponge in my chest.

Once Hitler turned his attention to Russia we did not always sleep in the dugout. At first my parents were apprehensive that bombers might return – and my march along the balcony on sentry duty did not reassure them. We were not directly in the path of the Baedeker raids[35] of 1942 but there were intermittent raids and bombers flying over throughout that year and the next. When we had warning sirens for several nights we returned to the dugout rather than being forced to leave our warm beds upstairs.

Some evenings, though, were spent in the dining room, the quiet broken by Pop's favourite band music or one of the regular comedy programmes on the wireless: ITMA, Much Binding in the Marsh. If Mog was at home she would read to me and then settle down to some needlework. She won a prize at the Women's Institute for a siren suit made from an old sweater of my father's. I don't think that Churchill's version had a hood but mine did. It was always ready by my bed to put on quickly over my pyjamas if we needed to go down to the shelter.

---

[35] In spring 1942, the German Air Force launched a series of destructive air raids against historic towns and cities in Britain. These attacks were named after the famous German travel guides.

And sometimes it was necessary. In November 1943 my father noted:

> Jan and I have been watching for searchlights and gunfire after the wireless went off about 7pm After ½ hour we saw a few gun flashes and after the sirens went there was some gunfire towards Hertford, but shortly after the all-clear went. Jan enjoys herself watching, wearing as she did tonight, her dressing gown, woollen leggings and tin-hat. Once she climbed on the dugout but was recalled by Florrie and I was choked off for want of better sense to let her do it. As I write this in the dugout, having decided to stay down, Jan is in bed having done some reading, Florrie is reading the paper, and Gran is knitting so what with the wireless we are quite quiet and warm. Now 8.30pm and we already feel sleepy.

I remember the searchlights flashing across the black arena of the sky, swooping and criss-crossing each other, the brilliance of the stars, the crisp night air and the pungent smell of the damped out bonfire.

And a week later in the diary:

> On coming up from the dugout early this morning it was very white but I expect the frost to go as the barometer is very still and inclined to fall. I was cold during the night, not being able to get really warm after 3am. It is nice to come up to a fire and a cup of tea. We used to go to bed for an hour or so but found that bed pulled so that it was better not to be tempted. Sometimes, in fact pretty often, I would like to have a good lie in bed for a night. As it happened, last night we could have done but there is always that chance of a raid which would probably mean going down.

Once a week, sometimes twice, my Dad would go to the cinema. He paid for advertisements for the business on the cinema screen. Slides of all the local firms were beamed up in the intermission and free tickets were part of the deal. I am not sure that many of the films were exciting – especially the "B" films for there were always two, but the programme changed on Thursdays so there was a choice. As a treat I went with him. I saw *In Which We Serve* in 1942 – a film that gave me a stiff upper lip and a naval bearing for days. And later I saw *The Life and death of Colonel Blimp* and *I know where I'm going*. Pathé news, heralded by its cockerel, was eagerly awaited, for I hoped to see Field Marshal Montgomery, who was my hero.

There was a slight downside to these companionable outings. My father always tried to sit at the end of a row as this enabled him – not a fervid republican but with a dislike of show – to slink up the aisle immediately the programme ended, followed by an embarrassed daughter. We would be through those squeaky doors as the clattering of the folding seats denoted the rising of the loyal audience for the national anthem.

I am not sure how he found space to lighten his life by playing football again. In February 1943 he recorded:

> On coming home from the pictures, which were *'Old Mother Riley'* and *Shanghai Gesture* – very poor both, I was told that Reg[36] had phoned to know if I would play football tomorrow at Welham Green for the Police v. RAF Woodhill. As I have no boots and it is doubtful if I have shirt or shorts, no decision was made. I would like to play, for it's such a time since the last game and after so many years of regular matches I'm anxious to visit more youthful things. The result, after five years' absence may be such that I'm better in retirement. We shall see.

---

[36] Reg Simmons, who had a bakery business in Hatfield. He and Randall were friends all their lives from babyhood.

The next day he continued

This morning I was hoping, although I made out that I did not care one way or the other, to be asked to play for certain. Well, I was, so there was a hunt round for kit. Mostly by Florrie. Mother said there was a pair of boots down there, which were Norm's, so I fetched them. The size was one larger than my usual but they seemed OK. A shirt? This is where we were stuck, but Florrie rescued the situation by borrowing one from Mr. Bennett, and after further search, the stockings and shorts were unearthed. Sid Hollier had a convenient journey to make to Welham Green so that Reg and I got a lift. On arrival it looked as though we were 12 men which I thought would rule me out but it was not so to my relief. The game was most enjoyable, no rough play and we won 4-2. Afterwards, well, I should say about half-time, age began to assert itself and limbs felt stiff and my wind was not what it was. I was pleased though that I could still play a fair game. Considering that most of our team is in their 30s and the RAF chaps are youngsters who should be fit, the win was surprising. We older chaps put plenty of go into it, although the kicking and passing were rather wild at times.

Recollections of the past came crowding in: the games we played for the Pirates. What good times they were. It seemed that those days would go on forever. After the Pirates I recollect some of the Hatfield Thursday games. But just before the war they ceased and until today I had not had a game since.

He turned out intermittently for the police who were always short of players and continued to play until he was nearly forty. I remember my mother dressing a nasty wound on

his shin and muttering that he was getting too old to play. He reluctantly took up bowls at the Hatfield Lawn Tennis and Bowling Club where his cousin Eric was already a keen player.
His diary in 1944 reveals anxiety about raids again.

> February 18th On coming from Home Guard I found it had been freezing. The paths were glassy which made walking in army boots a tricky business. In case we were dragged from our beds during the night we spread some salt on the steps to keep them clear of ice. (1 o'clock in the morning) "Is it guns?" said Florrie dreamily. On looking out the appearance and sounds were of a raid well under way. Hastily dressing we scooted down to the dugout. All of us, except Jan who luckily dropped off to sleep again, were shivering with shock and cold. The planes were overhead quite a lot and the doors shook several times. Then a "swish" brought us to a stop in living for a second. 4 bombs were heard. Sometimes later the All-Clear was heard. A number of fires could be seen. A drop of rum quietened our shaking stomachs and apart from cat disturbances we slept until 6.30am.

As the war dragged on army convoys occasionally drove past. Canadian troops stopped for a break one day and every household offered mugs of tea. The soldiers hoisted children up into the jeeps and armoured vehicles, giving them chewing gum, letting them try on their tin hats.
And then followed the hope and optimism of D-Day.

> June, 6th 1944: A night disturbed by planes, the reason for this was explained by Florrie calling up to me just after 8am to say "It's started." Today is the day, awaited for so long, of the invasion of Europe. Until midday there was a

continuous stream of planes, mostly bombers, across the grey, clouded sky.

But three weeks later:
The weather is still very depressing and what with continual raids everywhere everyone is very weary. Of course, other areas around London and on the South coast must be much worse and one hears of people getting no sleep for nights on end. Also it is interfering with business. The lack of goods from London in the last two weeks has been most noticeable.

The wireless was turned on all day to hear the latest news. I found it exciting but I realised that my parents' hopes were muted by anxiety and worry for the casualties and loss of life. Norman was not involved in the Normandy invasion, he had spent time in Cyprus and the Middle East. My father would try to work out where he was from his brief and carefully worded letters and then would fulfil his requests for money. Joan, his sister, who had joined the ATS in 1941, was not sent abroad. Wanting to be a driver she was told she was not strong enough and reluctantly joined the pay corps based at Winchester. However, the progress of friends of my father and several of our assistants at that time was worry enough.

Another memory was standing on our flat roof and seeing the whole sky filled with planes drawing gliders, a seemingly never ending stream. My father again:

17th September 1944: This morning there started an armada which thrilled and excited us all as we watched for nearly two hours a procession of gliders, transports and planes carrying paratroops. At times there were fifty to a hundred in view at once. We guessed that Holland was the destination which was confirmed on the 6 o'clock

news. In two instances we saw gliders become detached from their towing planes. This afternoon the planes returned. Jan, Dad and I went for a walk this evening and saw a huge red sun sinking below the western horizon. It has been a beautiful, mellow day made noisy by machines.
The passing over of the armada was continued for three days. On Wednesday evening in the gathering darkness we saw two flights of about fifty pass over with their lights on, green, red and yellow. It was a fantastic and surprisingly beautiful sight.

After the excitement and hopes hanging on D-Day the V1 s, or doodle-bugs, were disrupting our lives.

16th June: We heard the rocket planes were in use over here last night which accounted for the terrific noise and explosions during the night The alert was on from 11o'clock till 9.30 this morning.
24th September: Have you seen one? (Doodlebug)' No! That was at 8.30 this evening but ten minutes later I had. It was roaring over the Bowls Club as I came out of Charlie Moore's having had my hair cut. I crossed the road came through the garden gate and lay down by the hedge. Then as it was still going, I got up and ran down the path, lay down by the shed and got up again. The engine stopped. There was a flash, followed by a terrific crack. I reached the dugout door which Florrie was holding open and dashed in. It was petrifying while it lasted though it could only have been a few seconds. It fell on Selwyn Crescent. Four killed, many injured and the damage considerable. It left everybody a bit shaken this morning.

In the dugout, we could hear the wretched machine roaring nearer and knew that my father would be on his way home. When Mog had opened the door I heard the pounding of Pop's feet coming down the entrance. It was a nasty moment. By this time I was old enough to be frightened. We were spending nights regularly in the dugout and though my mother tried to make everything as calm and routine as she could I always felt a sense of foreboding as I put down my book – probably an encyclopaedia or a book by Arthur Ransome -, turn out the light and wait, not for sleep but for the siren.

The doodlebug that fell on Selwyn Crescent was the first of nearly thirty attacks in the Hatfield area by V1s and V2s. It scared me: the danger too close. Hardly had the funeral services for those who died in Selwyn Crescent than a doodlebug fell even nearer home in the early morning of 10th October. The explosion shook the dugout; indeed it shook my bed and we all woke in terror. The bomb had fallen on St Audrey's Senior school near the railway destroying many houses in two roads nearby, trapping many people inside their homes, the Council offices, the police station and, of course, the school. My father recorded:

> Tuesday 10th The early hours of the morning again brought tragedy, sorrow and destruction when a flying bomb fell near the railway. Dad and I went to the branch at 5.30am to clear up but, apart from the windows being smashed and the stock on the floor, there was little damage. The shops opposite were in a bad state. Worst was the casualties, 8 being killed, several of whom were well known to me, Steve Curtis, his wife and son, also Don Purdee.

Bread was sent over to 101 from Simmons the Baker very early to be sliced on our bacon machines and the assistants were quickly mobilized to make sandwiches with Spam for which we had special permits. Mog was quickly called out with the Red Cross to offer aid. My father and grandfather also made a donation of food and tea to the Carmelite Convent where breakfasts and dinners were offered to those who had no cooking facilities. Apparently the entire town rallied and acted with speed, commonsense and courage.

Later Mog took me to see the damage. The grimy, gritty smell of charred wood, smoke and chaos was unbelievable. Firemen, residents were working in grim silence to clear the wreckage. A sad, depressed atmosphere pervaded the whole town; the daily chatter in the shops quiet and sober, and people moved quickly about their business. Two days later:

> Thursday 12th Raids are becoming regular and the strain accentuated by the two recent tragedies is beginning to show on people's manner and speech. The ideals of victory pale before the urgent wish for a speedy end, especially after the recent wave of optimism.
> 55[St. Albans Rd], considering the close proximity to the bomb escaped very well and the only damage was a broken back door. Here at 101 we had one front window out. We were lucky. One dreads the night coming and this feeling is shared by all. After five years we are weary of it and the strain has become almost overbearing at times. Today I have had one of my heads which has laid me low.

At that time, and I don't know how we came to acquire them, we were given a pile of American magazines – the equivalent of Good Housekeeping, Woman and Home. There were colourful advertisements depicting mothers in frilly aprons and high-heeled shoes dolling out luxurious food to scrubbed and shining children in smart kitchens; cheerful farmers in bright checked shirts riding on enormous new tractors; fathers in large cars. They seemed to come from another world. Towards the end of the war everything in Britain seemed so drab and grey. It is impossible to convey the wonder I felt as I pored over the magazines in bed.

After the late autumn of 1944 the entries in my father's diary are sparse and laconic. It seems that the "weariness and strain" had indeed affected him. His end of year entry said:

Sunday 31st During the past year the Home Guard has stood down which at least signifies the passing of the possibility of invasion. In June I was graded 3 at a medical. Norm has been overseas for over two years during which he has been in several countries. Joan has been home for three months while Mother's leg was bad. Two terrifying incidents in Sept. and Oct. killed 12 people here and did a good deal of damage. The weather has been fair with no extremes although we have had rather more fog than usual. And so in a few hours we pass into 1945 with hope for peace, good health and thankfulness for what we have been able to pass through.

Snow and power cuts blighted the winter of '45 but despite the privation there was some growing optimism. Sledges came out and families enjoyed tobogganing on slopes in Hatfield Park. Then spring came and the war in Europe ended.

On 3rd May Pop's diary read:

This evening I saw pictures of the Belsen concentration camp.

4th: Fighting on the Western Front has practically ceased today and the Germans in Holland, Denmark and North Germany have capitulated.

5th: Have listened to the last "War Report" at the

end of the news, which was preceded by a news item concerning the Polish Question. Disturbing events are occurring in this matter and do not give a confident view of the future.

Then nothing. Nothing about celebration and mostly silence in his diary for the rest of the year. In his diary for 1944 he had often mentioned the reactions of townsfolk and customers to the renewed and frightening raids, recording their exhaustion. "When the engines of the doodle bugs stopped the world stopped too for a moment - and one's heart." So perhaps the effort of just carrying on was as much as he could manage[37].

What a shame we have no other account in the family. Why don't I remember that we were given two days off school, that bunting magically appeared all round the town, that there was a vast Victory bonfire in the Park on VE day? All that surfaces in my mind is a shapeless fizzy excitement.

That there were street parties I do know because in the shop we sliced the bread again on our bacon machines ("They were never as sharp again", swore my grandfather.) I was stood on a box to join the team in the Dispatch, smearing margarine on the slices of bread and passing them on to others who sparingly covered them with slices of Spam of which we had been allocated another extra supply.

The ending of the war in the Far East has more substance in my mind. Before the inevitable creation of more piles of sandwiches there were some significant events. On VJ night the residents of a nearby road were dancing in the streets to loud music from the wireless. My memory is of hearing the music while lying in bed enduring a sick headache. But things improved and I can't do better that quote Brian Lawrence:

---

[37] Perhaps too there was something of the same phlegmatic acceptance of life that we read recently in the diary of a farmer in Herefordshire: 8th May, 1945: Today saw the cessation of war with Germany. Planted peas.

The next afternoon street parties were held throughout the town and in the Park 'over 2400 children were given a big tea with sandwiches cakes, buns, fruit, sweets, nuts and dates, with mugs of lemonade to help it down. They ran races with especial Victory zest'…Later there was dancing around the 30ft high bonfire to music broadcast from a van lent by de Havilland's. The following Sunday there was a Victory parade in the afternoon from the North Front of Hatfield House to the Parish Church followed by a service of thanksgiving.

I am almost certain that I did not attend the tea in the park. Why not? But my parents did take me to the bonfire in the evening. Huge crackling bursts of orange flame rose in the evening sky celebrating the buoyant atmosphere of unimaginable relief.

On the Sunday Gran Hope and I walked to the North Front of the Park to watch the parade. The Home Guard was presumably there although I don't remember seeing my father. I suspect he managed to avoid it. Seeing my mother in the ranks of the Red Cross is all I remember of the Parade. Why is memory so odd in its selection of events? I remember standing with Gran. I remember the drooping lushness of the lime trees in the avenue. I remember the crowds, but the marching, the soldiers, the band: all gone, all evaporated. The memories of spreading slices of bread with margarine, counting coupons, playing with a rifle, pursuing Hitler on a chair still remain alive and real.

Chapter 8

Another happy childhood

Godmother Nell gave me a kaleidoscope for my eighth birthday. Peering down the eyepiece at the brightly coloured pieces, I would shake it vigorously and see the patterns miraculously change to something new. I can't think of a better way to describe my childhood memories. As I record them they change, fall into different shapes and patterns with little regard for time. Mog created patchwork cushions and bedcovers and they too are like my memories: people and places jostle up against one another like the varied patches cut from my old dresses.

My childhood was certainly coloured and affected by the war but much of it was just the simple childhood of the 1940s and would have been little different had there been no war at all. There would have been more sweets, a holiday or two. We might have had a car. But children would still have played hopscotch and five stones, listened to Children's Hour, gone to parties and played musical chairs. Childhood would still have been unsophisticated and unspoilt by the pressures of advertising and the urgency to grow up fast.

Seeing myself through my father's eyes as he described me in his diaries, I suspect I was a quaint little thing and because I was an only child until I was ten years old, my oddities were not shaped and rubbed off by siblings.

12th August, 1943: Janet has discovered that she has 16 faces. This was the result of gazing in the mirror as is her practice when getting up in the mornings. Florrie, wondering why she was so long in getting dressed, crept to the bedroom and heard "No, I have had that one" which was no doubt the result of a trial for number 17.

I still make faces in the mirror deploring my wrinkles.

I was somewhat officious. Setting potatoes and beans in my own patch of garden I declared it was private and that anyone found on it without permission would be fined 6d. Sanctimonious, too: When hearing on the radio that Hitler said "Pray for peace" I commented at the age of seven: "He'd be better off if he prayed for forgiveness".

Stamp collecting was encouraged by my father who was a keen collector of British and Empire Stamps, but collecting matchbox covers was my own initiative and Pop looked out for specimens too for in those days the box covers were many and varied. Going to school on the bus when I was nine I gazed longingly at a little old woman who sat on the settee seats opposite, lighting her cigarette with a match from a box whose cover I coveted. "Ask her if you can have it when she has finished up the matches," suggested my mother, but I was not brave enough. Before the passion waned I had a full album but it disappeared long ago[38].

I did not learn to read early but, encouraged by my parents, books soon became a passion. From *The Tale of Peter Rabbit* and all the other stories by Beatrix Potter, tales like *Ameliaranne and the Green Umbrella*[39] I moved on to the volumes kept from his childhood by my father: *Children of the New Forest*, *Settlers in Canada* or Mog's copy of *Little Women*. New books were hard to come by so I supplemented them by visits to Daisy Grey, a lady who had a shop in Old Hatfield. She sold mainly stationery, like pen nibs at ½d each, toys and newspapers but I had eyes only for the secondhand books. I would take books that I thought I had grown out of, get a few

---

[38] When I was teaching I asked a cherubic small boy of seven what his interests were. In a piping voice he said confidently: "Astronomy and Palaeontology. My father interested me in Astronomy but I think I have interested him in Palaeontology. My interests were not so academic.

[39] Constance Heward's 1920s tales of the Stiggins family

pennies for them and then browse amongst the titles of the books stacked on the damp and dusty shelves. There I found Garry Hogg's Explorer stories; Castle Blair[40] by Flora Shaw and read avidly the story of the wealthy and unruly Irish family, high on adventure and short on parental control – like so many children's books of the time. A dog-eared and battered copy of Black Beauty bought there was read again and again. Deep misery would overcome me when I read some of the sadder episodes:

> A short time after this a cart with a dead horse in it passed our cab-stand. The head hung out of the cart-tail, the lifeless tongue was slowly dropping with blood; and the sunken eyes! But I can't speak of them, the sight was too dreadful.

No sparing of children's feelings. I would turn back the pages to read about Ginger and Black Beauty in their happier days together before I could go to sleep.

Half-term and holiday treats were visits to St Albans or Welwyn Garden City to purchase a new book by Malcolm Saville or the later stories of Arthur Ransome. I would read long after lights out by using a torch under the bedclothes when we were sleeping in the flat.

Curiosity was encouraged by my parents. My father recorded:

> 11th November 1943: Jan and I went for a walk this evening in the moonlight. As we started a big full moon was rising out of a slight mist into a bright starlit sky. As

---

[40] First published in 1877, *Castle Blair* was translated into several languages and continued to be extremely popular in the UK and US well into the 20th century. It was based on Flora Shaw's Anglo-Irish childhood experiences. Astonishing life story – look her up.

we walked she noticed the length of our shadows which started a series of questions as to how tall would I be if I was as tall as that lamp post pointing to one in St Albans Rd, and if I was as tall as that and she remained the size she was, how far up my legs would she come. Good fun and we both enjoyed ourselves.

Mog both entered into my fantasies and encouraged practical skills. She built a doll's house for me and together we made chairs out of small ice cream tubs cut to shape and chests of drawers from matchboxes. The making was enjoyable but I fear I did not play much with the finished article.

Neither parent was in the least concerned that I was a tom–boy. In 1943 Pop wrote:
Janet has been playing the piano and has now gone down into the garden to indulge in a game of fancy. I wonder who she is now: a cowboy, lumberjack or dispatch rider? Perhaps all in turn. Never a girl's game but always pretending. Perhaps the cat is a lion being chased.

It still surprises me that they did not seem to mind that their small daughter mostly scorned dolls and was not keen on parties or pretty dresses. I suspect that there was little excitement in pretending to be an Indian squaw or a soldier's wife. Men had all the adventures. They knew my fantasy that I was the son of Field Marshal Montgomery, indeed they called him "Dad" too. Dolls only interested me if they could be bandaged or put into hospital. Mainly I was fascinated by the

Wild West and had a cowboy suit given me for Christmas. If Red Indians were involved however, I was almost always on their side. I was given lead cowboys and Indians – I think with nostalgia of the stagecoach with four galloping horses, cowboy driver and guard with little metal pegs in their bottoms to anchor them to the seat and with tiny trunks and packages on the roof. And I had a fort guarded by a nineteenth century regiment, brave in red coats and helmets.

Somehow my father managed to acquire a Hornby Train set. Perhaps it was his wish to have a son made him search so hard. The exciting long box was waiting for me on Christmas day, 1943. Inside was the royal blue engine, Sir Nigel Gresley and its tender, three carriages, a set of rails and buffers all slotted into the shaped recesses of the cardboard. It was both elegant and exciting and we played with it for hours, sometimes interrupted by a cat who tried to knock the engine off the rails.

Our cats were forbearing companions. Jim was black with white bib and paws and joined the household when I was two. As a kitten he broke his leg and was confined to an empty tea chest until it healed. I would stand on tiptoe to look over the top at the small mite sitting quietly at the bottom. Pooh, my patient tabby and white cat, was given to me when I was four. I used to dress him in dolls' clothes and take him for walks in the dolls' pram. Left to himself he would sit very still beneath birds' nests in the hawthorn hedge, making little mewing sounds hoping that one or other of the nestlings would become sufficiently agitated to fall out into his waiting mouth. He was impervious to the wiles of Phyllis, one of the shop cats. She would make up to him, roll on her back and crawl on her belly, flashing her eye lashes lasciviously while he looked on with supreme indifference. Grandpa called Pooh 'The Ornament' because he was frightened of mice and if put into a tea chest where a nest had been found, would leap out and disappear for the day. Despite this failing, and for their safety, the cats were put into the storehouses at night. It became a nightly source of fun when the tiniest rattle of my father's keys would cause the cats to slink under the sideboard or rush into a bedroom to hide under a bed.

There was a succession of more predatory felines kept to catch the inevitable mice in the storehouses and shop. There was Tiger, a, bullet-headed Tom with the torn cauliflower ears of a fighter. Occasionally he would creep up the steps to our flat to seek warmth in the kitchen and once he reprehensibly bedewed a table leg with pungent wee. A neighbour coming into the house that day said appreciatively to Mog "Ah, making blackcurrant jam, eh?" Mog did not enlighten her. Ginny, tortoiseshell and white, was a good mouser much favoured by my grandfather. She had several litters many of which were born in a comfortable cardboard box lined with a blanket under the bench of the Dispatch.

Once when she was very near her time, she disappeared and I was worried. I asked the MacSweeneys and the Dawsons next door if I could look in their gardens but there was no sign of her. "Do you think she could have gone far as Auntie May's"? I asked my father fearfully. He smiled. "You should go and ask her", he replied, wondering if I had the courage. Screwing it to the utmost I went down the dark passage way to her front door and knocked. I heard steps coming down and nearly ran away. The door opened just a crack and her thin wrinkled face peered out, "What do you want?" I managed to explain and she agreed I could go round the back to look. Courage rewarded: there was Ginny with a litter of four squidgy pink kittens in a nest of long grass amidst the unkempt raspberry bushes.

In those days there were always wandering tomcats so overproduction of kittens was a problem. Benny Bishop would arrive on his creaky bicycle, lean it against a wall in the yard and take a large sack from a cardboard box strapped on the back. With no consideration for hygiene he placed the sack on the bench in the dispatch. Male kittens to be kept were caught, thrust into the sack. Benny's hands would follow holding a sharp implement. A sharp little miaow and out would come the emasculated kitten, wiped clean and sent off. I watched, mystified.

Besides the cats I had a white rabbit, naturally called Peter. I suspect my mother cleaned him out more often than I did and occasionally, I am ashamed to say, I forgot to feed him. I was better with my guinea pigs though they suffered a high casualty rate.

12th August: A tragedy to report. Guinea pig baby disappeared over night. Conclusion is that it fell out of the hutch and in fright squeaked which attracted a cat. We think it was Phyllis. Having examined the size of our cats' stomachs we have deduced, rightly or wrongly that it wasn't in either Pooh or Jim.

At one time Mr. Hall, the head gardener of Hatfield House gave me two doves. We had a bird house on a tall pole ready for them. "Keep them in for a few days," advised Mr. Hall "feed them well and they will soon learn to fly round and come back to their house." We did as he said and after a week opened the door. They came out, shook their wings, rose into the air and flew unerringly in the direction of Hatfield House. Mr. Hall did not give up. He produced another a few weeks later but I fear that she, more domestically inclined, fluttered down on to the ground to try the chickens' food rather than fly. She was stalked and eaten by one of the cats. Children with pets quickly learn about life and death.

All our animal food was made from scratch. The cats had the scrapings from our plates – and that wasn't much, plus bacon rind, fish heads, crusts and Bovril. They did well enough and presumably we expected them to supplement their wartime diet in the traditional way of cats. Rabbits and guinea pigs had carrots, cabbage leaves and meal and we always gathered dandelions, plantains and other weeds when we were out walking.

I longed for a pony of my own, but did I ever seriously expect to own one? I don't think so. I compensated by enjoying the hobby horses which my mother made by stuffing old socks enhanced with felt eyes and ears, fastened securely on old broomsticks. They were stabled in the garden shed and I won many rosettes when jumping them over sticks and boxes placed round the paths in the garden. This occupation was magnified and built upon with my own children. At one time Kate and Nell had over fifteen hobby horses. Like Mog, I fashioned them from old socks though sometimes when the worn heels gave way and the broomsticks protruded, Kate would announce that Hengest or Horsa had "unicorn disease".

Occasionally Mr. Savage would offer me a short ride from French Horn Lane to the blacksmith's near the cinema. Always dressed in breeches and riding boots when with a horse, he was a cheerful man, with a smile that went right up to his twinkling eyes. He lived at the lodge of the Old Rectory where he worked as a gardener, but his love was for horses. He had been Stud Groom at Walkern Hall, near Stevenage, working for Miss Georgina Cotton Brown. He would tell me stories of how, wearing a top hat and livery jacket, he used to ride with his employer in Rotten Row and stay in Park Lane during the season to look after the horses[41]. At the blacksmiths I was fascinated by the roaring red fire, the hammering and the salty burning smell as the shoe was applied to the horse's hoof.

---

[41] At the age of 81 he hunted twice a week with the Enfield Chace Hunt, immaculate in black jacket and bowler.

When I was eight my patient father hired a pony from a livery stable in Park Street on a Sunday afternoon and he would lead it with me precariously on its back up beside the railway to Travellers' Lane bridge and round though the lanes. We did not always get that far. The usual pony was Josephine, a curmudgeonly creature. My father learned to take a pocketful of carrots which would sometimes persuade her to amble though never to stride out. From the age of nine I used to go to a riding school at Hertingfordbury with Sid and Frank Hollier, their mother would take us. Halcyon afternoons were enjoyed, saddling and grooming the ponies, riding through the lanes and fields. Sid, Frank and I would vie to ride Peter a small grey pony with some spirit in him, but later Zephyr, a handsome dappled grey, was my favourite mount.

I suspect I was happiest playing alone. Supplementary uses of the dugout illustrate that. At my request, my Dad leaned a wooden ladder against the green mound of the dugout. It probably became my ship after I had seen Noel Coward on the bridge of *In Which We Serve*. I hauled up pieces of wood and old cardboard boxes and placed them on the concrete roof of the entrance to form the Captain's bridge. I used my small telescope to survey the surrounding ocean and ordered the guns to be run out. Sometimes I helped myself to chicken meal and made little cakes which I dried out on the concrete ready for a Red Indian feast, or crawled up the steep side just raising my head above the top looking warily for the enemy. The grass on the dugout was shaggy, coarse and bleached. I lay on the top and watched birds scribbling the sky – which in memory was always blue. Pooh would emerge sleepily from a warm nest of grass under the shade of the plum tree and sit beside me thoughtfully washing his paws. I think of those days as being gloriously silent, the air only occasionally shattered by the sound of planes.

Forgetting the war, the dugout featured in Treasure Island

or Swiss Family Robinson, or became a castle where I waged war against besiegers. My Dad, not generally a good craftsman, made a catapult for me from a smoothed piece of forked wood, strong elastic and a piece of leather to hold the stone. I suppose I was firmly instructed to use it safely and never near the ducks, chickens or cats and it never caused mayhem. Less potentially lethal was a cap revolver – a treasured gift for my seventh birthday – which when fired gave off a thrilling whiff of gunpowder. My "pretend" games were thorough in their execution, and whatever character I was playing required my parents to enter in to the game wholeheartedly. Our older daughter insisted upon the same attention to detail in her games. Many a time Nell would be reproved for forgetting her part while Kate knew every room in the castle where they, the two princesses lived, or the names of the horses in the royal stables – and their ancestry.

The dugout was positioned in the orchard with two plum trees on one side and a number of apple and pear trees on the other. My Dad fixed up a long fat pole between the plum trees. With a folded blanket on it and reins attached to a rising branch in front, I rode across the prairie for hours, lassoed cattle and then, finding a place to bivouac, would dismount, make a small fire nearby and bake small potatoes in the ashes and cook "dampers" – grey ashy twists of flour and water on a stick which my long suffering parents would come to eat.

Our small menagerie provided both occupation and entertainment. Besides my pets, and the cats we kept chickens and a few Muscovy ducks, black and white with pink beaks. The first heavy lumbering drake was called James Pig (christened by me and I know not why) Subsequent drakes merely had ordinal numbers after the name like royalty. The ducks had various names but I only remember Custard and Pinky. Seeing James Pig clambering on top of Custard and wriggling round to position himself, I enquired of Mog what he was doing. She explained. "I hope gentleman don't do that to ladies" I replied primly.

Unlike most ducks the Muscovys were good mothers and sat on their eggs with commendable patience hatching out batches of delightful fluffy brown and yellow ducklings. The ducks often laid eggs under the thick privet hedge surrounding the garden and passing school children occasionally filched eggs through the fence. Dad made a small pond lined with concrete in the orchard, and very quickly the ducklings would jump into the water and skitter about, watched with horror from the edge by our sedate, landlubber Light Sussex hens. One hot day my cousin, Josie and I tucked our dresses into our knickers and joined the ducks. The bottom of the pond was full of excrement and mud and felt deliciously squelchy between our toes. Caught by my mother we were rushed upstairs to be cleaned.

My father rarely managed to clip the ducks' wings sufficiently short, so the birds roosted in the apple trees and frequently flew out into the lane. An entertainment for the locals in the Robin Hood pub across the road on a summer night was to watch the ducks circling the orchard and across the lane. Dad reported in his diary:

> After a while it was decided to eat James Pig as food was not very plentiful. We did not tell Janet. The flesh of game birds though is quite dark and when the dinner appeared on the table Janet looked at it suspiciously and said "That's James Pig" None of us could eat him.

When I was seven we went to the Mill Green Lodge of the Park and bought from the keeper an Old English Game bantam and her ten, tiny multi coloured chicks. A run was made and I looked after my bantams carefully. In due time the hens laid a good supply of their small eggs which I would sell to our shop assistants. One cockerel, Billy had to be disposed of. He was a ferocious little bird who, as soon as we entered the big run where all the chickens and ducks were kept, would rush over, flapping his wings threateningly and peck any part of our anatomy he could reach.

My father encouraged me to garden. I had a small plot of my own. I think I sowed seeds so thickly that very few came up at all but I enjoyed trundling my little red wheelbarrow round the paths, helping to weed and enjoying the excitement of a bonfire. Best of all was picking young pea pods and eating the tiny, juicy peas or, well hidden by the tall canes, choosing the best raspberries for private enjoyment.

If I could not play in the garden or wanted other distraction there was always the shop. When Ossie, Miss Osborne, the lass who ran the office was called up early in 1942 my mother took on her work. I would sit in the office and draw. I helped or hindered the assistants in packing sugar or stacking tins, watched the men delivering flour in sacks with flaps in the back of their white hats, their coats and faces all white. Sometimes I would climb up the rough hessian sacks of dry goods in the warehouse, find a hollow amongst the cardboard boxes and sit driving a tank into battle or sail a boat to a deserted shore.

By eight or nine years old one of my occasional tasks on a Sunday morning was to tidy and clean the large glass lined cupboard behind the main counter that held patent medicines. Precariously standing on the counter I would neaten the rows of Zam Buk healing ointment, the bottles of Scott's Emulsion – a green viscous fluid which I loathed being given in the winter as a supplement. It rubbed shoulders' with Parish's Chemical Food, Carter's little liver pills and camphorated oil in blue ridged bottles. I can still conjure up the medicated smell that wafted out when I opened the cupboard doors.

In good weather I would sit with Diggler Cannon while he

scraped the canvas skin off the cheddar cheeses. He would tell me tall stories in between puffs at his short smelly pipe. He kept up his habit of teasing we Tingey children. The job of Poppy Hopkins, he said, was making pips to put in raspberry jam. He did not frighten me with tales of lions and tigers but was ready with a puzzling answer to my questions. An early pre-war memory is being hoisted up on to the counter on a Sunday morning by one of the male assistants and persuaded to recite nursery rhymes and they would tease and joke. Once war ensued and most of the men were called up and only three elderly chaps, Josh, Mr. Powers and Diggler were left, I suspect I was a nuisance to them.

My father, in order to vary his week, used to deliver the groceries all round Hatfield Park and in the holidays I used to go with him. The van was old and the narrow roads rough and potholed but I enjoyed the trips. As well as taking the groceries, Pop would note down the order for the following week. I had my regular small treats at the various houses. At Mrs. Maddocks I would commune with Judy, the small black Labrador belonging to the keeper. At Mill Green Mrs. Titmuss would find some biscuits and on a fine day I liked to watch the stream cascading under the mill. At some of the more gentrified houses I would stay in the van and read.

Other times spent with my father were usually on a Sunday and sometimes on Thursday afternoons when the shop was closed. He would play games with my Indians and Cowboys, take me for walks, enter into my fantasies, prepared to be Bouncer, my horse or when we walked in the park we would hunt cattle thieves.

5th February, 1943: In the afternoon we went for a walk up the old lane and collected the chips of wood which we had seen on Thursday. Janet came home with a bundle of wood tied with a handkerchief on her shoulder. She said she was a cowboy bringing home wood for the old camp fire.

During 1944 I learned to ride a bicycle. I had been hinting that I wanted a bike for a while but they were difficult to come by. In September Pop went to St Albans in answer to an advertisement but was disappointed for he reckoned "it was little more than a 'fairy cycle', in bad condition and at a ridiculous price of £8." A month later one was found and it was the beginning of many happy hours spent with my father. I soon learned to wobble along with the support of an occasional hand on the saddle but for a while had extreme difficulty in dismounting. This was overcome by Pop riding up beside me and holding on to the saddle while I got off. Eventually I mastered the art and early on Sunday mornings we would ride long miles on the quiet lanes around Hatfield sometimes pausing to hunt for mushrooms or pick blackberries in season. One morning we ventured on the great North Road and were amazed to see what appeared to be a cycling club but realized it was about thirty German prisoners, mostly in red sweaters, out for a ride with one small British soldier as a guard. "Don't think he would have much hope of catching them", commented Pop.

Mog was the anchor of the family though certainly no inert or heavy one. She was lively, and would probably have been even livelier had my father not been sometimes quiet and not eager for company. She was active, as I have described and could extract humour out of her encounters with neighbours, customers, and events. She could be sharp in her comments on people, sharp and forthright, but in a way that usually ended in laughter. If really riled with someone she would express it in her own totally original way "O pot on him!" she would say emphatically. I have never been able to work out where she got that from. Do you suppose it might emanate from chamber pots being emptied from an upstairs window? In her later years the sharpness went and she developed such generosity of spirit and a latent sense of mischief which pleasured all who knew her. She never appeared anxious or fearful. She must have been at times but no doubt hid that from me. She too entered whole heartedly into my games. One winter she damaged her knee in the snow. I was sliding on my sledge down the little slope in Dog Kennel Lane. "I'll show you", she said confidently, careered down on her tummy on the sledge, rolled off and damaged one knee sufficiently to need crutches for a while.

At home in the evenings both my parents read and told me stories when they were not trying to win the war. Dad had a good line in Hoppy and Sammy stories – the adventures of two small squirrels, which could last for nearly an hour.

> February, 1943: This evening I was coaxed into telling a Hoppy story. I admit I quite enjoyed telling it to Jan who was thrilled and several times joined in with suggestions as to what mischief Hoppy and Sammy should get into next.

My mother spun excellent yarns about Moosh, one of the shop cats, a black with white bib, nose and paws. According to Mog she wore a white flying suit and helmet like Amy Johnson and had a Tiger Moth which used to land on the flat roof. The government called her out at short notice if rations were being eaten by rats and she would go into action, rising into the sky, a mere speck and arrive home next morning with great tales to tell.

Before I was sent off to bed my evenings were quiet but companionable, especially in the years between the Blitz and the Doodlebugs. When Mog and Pop were out I always had Gran Hope. She helped me to cut out a picture of a small boy from a women's magazine and we made cut out clothes for him fastened with folded tabs at the shoulder. I also had a stable of horses cut out from Country Life and pasted on to cardboard, their names written on the back. It was in 1943 that Pop wrote

> Janet found some of our Xmas club cards in the office and decided we should all save each week. But her idea of a club was more comprehensive than ours so this evening she came down into the office and asked me to come upstairs soon as it was Club night. On arriving upstairs I found she had arranged that we should play games: Table tennis, Tiddlywinks and "I spy" for an hour. Anyway, we all enjoyed it.

It was a pastime that lasted intermittently for the whole winter.

On Sunday evenings Mog and I would accompany Gran Hope, who was a keen churchgoer, to St Luke's, the small Newtown church where my father had pumped the organ as a boy. There I would gaze at the wooden war memorial on the wall commemorating the dead of the First World War and note the names of my great uncles, or peruse the Tables of affinity in the front of the Book of Common Prayer telling me who I could not marry. Sometimes my interest would be caught by a Bible lesson well read or the words of a hymn rousingly sung. But the sermons rarely appealed, the organ creaked and whined and the choir was not mellifluous. There was one lady whose voice soared flutingly over the others. Mog nicknamed her "Mrs. Whoops"! Church meant community more than worship – as it so often does. The congregation worked together at festivals and kept neighbourly eyes on each other. Mog used to "do" the flowers for Christmas and Easter and I would go with her, rooting out sour smelling vases from the vestry and filling them from the tap outside. Mog was skilled at flower decoration but did not like to get involved with the rivalry that often assails flower ladies.

What of private religion? My mother was assiduous in getting me when small to kneel to say my prayers before getting into bed.

> Thank you for the world so sweet
> Thank you for the food we eat
> Thank you for the birds that sing
> Thank you God, for everything.

Not a bad start. After all it was a thirteenth century monk, Meister Eckhart, who said: "If the only prayer you ever say in your entire life is thank you it will be enough."

Mog was not one to push religion on to her children. Nor was my father. When I was a teenager and aired strong religious opinions, he would often say "Ah, but..." and put the other point of view. As a child I enjoyed books of Bible stories with pop-up pictures and am grateful that they gave me good background knowledge. At that time, there was still a general acceptance of Christian belief and churchgoing. It was knitted into the fabric of life and went unquestioned. More important for my subsequent life was my parents' enjoyment of the world, of small things: showing me a broken robin's egg found in the grass, going out to see a sunset, or getting me up to see a sky stuffed with stars, or a huge harvest moon, reading poetry and listening to music. It was indeed a happy childhood.

Chapter 9.

Out and About.

Being an only child until my brother was born in 1946, I suspect I was a little spoilt, there being no one else to share the limelight, though I did not always get my own way. And although I was teased by the assistants in the shop, I did not experience the rough and tumble of other children. When I went to school I found it hard to fit in. Other children did not want to play the imaginary games of which I was so fond.

There were few children living near us – other than Maureen MacSweeney next door - and those living up the Right of Ways opposite. They went to a different school and I presume that neither my parents nor theirs ever considered our meeting. As I have said before the Tingeys were small trout in a pond of minnows and there was not the opportunity to meet other children at non-existent playgroups or nurseries. My mother's best friend, René, had a daughter and we would play in a desultory manner with my dolls if she and her mother came over for tea; and Brian, the son of the cashier at the shop occasionally came to play, but I did not have close friends as a child.

My mother had grown up with a gang of her peers, had a brother, met boys, learned the hurly-burly of the playground. Our girls lacked a brother but they went to mixed schools, played in the close where we lived with a dozen boys and girls of assorted ages. Kate, at five years old, was engaged for a whole summer to Matthew, a charming little boy who lived nearby and at seven she announced that a new boy at school kept looking at her. "I'm like the animals", she said grandiloquently, "I go to sleep in the winter and wake up to mate in the spring." Nell and her best friend David used to bath together until his mother and I wondered when they would decide to stop. Seven year old Nell stood at the top of the stairs in her nightie and fluttered her eyes. "David," she called alluringly, striking a pose. "I'm ready."

I did, however, spend some happy hours with the Hollier boys. Their father, Sid, was a good friend of my dad. They had known each other since boyhood and played football together. Their home was Goldings Dairy in French Horn Lane which was a favourite destination for a walk when I was small. There we could buy a small tub of cream or extra milk from the small shop at the entrance to the dairy. At the back of a yard was a range of buildings where some of the Guernsey cows were stalled. I was sometimes allowed to go in to watch the brown-eyed heifers suckling tiny Bambi-like calves and to savour the steamy, milky smell.

Frank, Sid and I sometimes played with their toy farm in the old farmhouse. We swopped our Britain's lead cows so that they had a herd of Guernseys like their father's while I increased my black and white Friesians. Sometimes their games were more daring than I fancied. We once climbed up into the loft that ran the whole length of one barn. We clambered through the hay until we reached an open window at the end. Frank found a short ladder which he poked through it until it reached the corresponding window in the next building. He and Sid fearlessly crawled across and urged me on. Terrified, my knees wobbling I managed to follow them. After all, I was a year older than Frank and could not lose face.

My Dad failed to record in his diary my dislike of parties. Such events were simple affairs: jellies and iced buns, jam and paste sandwiches, flabby pink blancmange. The parents put effort into games like Pass the Parcel and Musical Chairs. One summer afternoon I was invited to a party in Selwyn Drive – quite a way out of Hatfield - so I suppose my mother took me on the bus. How I hated sitting on the wooden draining board in the kitchen and having my knees scrubbed, they being grubby from playing in the sandpit. Gran Hope fussed a little. "Let's have a look at your nails" she would order. "Thought so: you could grow potatoes in them" That fault being remedied she put on my clean white socks and polished Clarke's sandals – what else would a '40s child wear? There were games in the garden and even now the smell of Leylandii takes me back to that afternoon where I hid between the thick bushes in the garden to avoid joining in.

I have no memory of my own birthday celebrations. Certainly I had many well-wishers. Mog kept all the cards from my first to my sixth birthday in an album and they are many and varied, very different from the cards of today: Snow White's Dwarves encased in the shape of the birthday number, cheeky cartoons and, of course the lucky boy peeling a banana.

I became a Brownie when I was seven. Apparently I wrote a letter by myself asking to join and my father recorded that I seemed very keen. My parents were pleased because they were aware that having played so often by myself I did not find it easy to make friends.

5th May, 1943: Janet went to her first Brownie meeting tonight, something she has been looking forward to for almost a year. She was pleased when she came home with a card on which was the Brownie Promise and Motto which she has to learn by next week. She knows it already. She tells me she is in the Pixie patrol.
7th July Janet's first night in Brownie uniform, which was all laid out on her bed with hat tucked in shoulder bands in real army fashion. What a thrill for her at an age when occasions such as this loom so large in importance. On her arrival home I was handed her diary. No word was spoken but I realised that I was meant to open it and read something. This I did and noted: "Sew badge on." written in pencil. An important action to be performed which I

doubt needed to be noted in a diary as it was most unlikely it would slip her memory. The next thing that will give her great pleasure is a church parade which she hopes will be soon.

Our younger daughter, Nell, was also keen to become a Brownie and could not wait to put on her uniform. After three or four weeks, however, she said she did not want to go any more as it was boring. To be fair, the Brown Owl of the pack was near retirement and the activities were not exciting. We said that she would have to write and explain the situation. After some thought in her room she came down with a letter: "Dear Brown Owl, I am sorry but I will not be coming to Brownies any more. It was not quite what I expected." That has become a useful family saying.

I did make a friend, Greta Birchall, at Brownies. We did not meet very often for she lived at the other end of Hatfield and we went to different schools but we had some adventures together and it was a friendship which lasted into our time as guides.

Besides the Holliers boys and Greta I occasionally played with my cousins, Anne and Josie. Both were the children of Roly, my father's next brother in age. The family lived in Roe Green. My parents were not always close with them. My mother reckoned that Grandad favoured them more than us, instancing that when he bought us anything – a picture, a piano for me - it was only because he had bought them for the other family first. Was it so? Mog was protective of my father, but he did not seem aware of any adverse favouritism. He refers to Roly without rancour in his diary and was uncritically fond of his father. Anne was two years older than I, and her sister a year younger. We would mainly meet at our grandmother's, play games in the garden, picking the pods of lupins for peas which we pretended to cook using a toy stove and saucepans, using the Anderson shelter as our house.

It was Christmas 1941 when we produced our first entertainment. This event occupied us for weeks before Christmas. We would go to Grandmas and she let us use the sitting room for our rehearsals. Anne was, of course, in charge. When the weather grew cold Grandmas allowed us a small electric fire. The fire had an extra use. We would lay it on its back and place ice cream wafers, purloined from the family shop, upon the wire guard, so that they toasted to a golden dry crispness. A real treat. The entertainment became an annual event for several years.

My father typed out programmes for the first "Fifty Fivers" Variety performance.

    1.Dickory's Horse   by the entire company.
    2.A Gipsy Tambourine Dance by Miss Anne Tingey.
    3.Christopher Robin by the entire Company.
    4.Fairy on the Christmas Tree by Miss Anne Tingey.

After the interval Josie sang *Lavender's Blue, diddle, diddle.* I, a Karaoke singer before its invention, strummed a toy banjo while miming Stephen Foster's *My Old Kentucky Home* and *Camptown Races* played on a wind-up gramophone, while Anne danced to the music of Swan Lake. Oh, we were a talented trio. You would have known that by the prolonged applause.

Mog and I had one memorable outing with Anne, Josie and Aunt Millie, their mother. The two adults must have felt a great need for excitement and a complete change for they lashed out and bought tickets for The Dancing Years at the Adelphi theatre in London late in 1943. Dressed in our best clothes we walked to the station and sat in the waiting room on the heavy leather covered benches. The railway carriage was stuffy and smelt pungently of cigarette smoke. I remember the lurch of the bus as we clambered up the outside staircase at King's Cross and I can still see the stage, hear the songs and the mellifluous voice of Ivor Novello, but most vivid in my mind is the homeward journey. As the train drew near to Hatfield it speeded up and swept through the station. "Know anyone up North, Florrie?" asked Auntie Millie cheerfully and we three girls giggled excitedly as the train rushed on. To our disappointment it stopped merely at Welwyn Garden City and we had to wait an hour for a slow London bound train to take us home.

With Anne and Josie I attended Saturday morning pictures – the highlight of the week. I do not remember how often I went or how old I was when I was first allowed to go. I would walk up the St Albans Road to meet my cousins outside the Regent Cinema and we would join the queue of excited children as we processed up the steps and into the foyer to pay our 2d. Then through the squeaky swing doors we would push into the warm fuggy darkness that was raucous with shouts and laughter. What did we see? Cartoons, Robin Hood, Tarzan and cowboy films must have predominated. If ever a kiss appeared on screen all the little boys would boo, groan and roar in disgust. I believe there were some live shows – magicians, comedians and some audience participation but I have forgotten all those – probably because I was a shy child and would have hated to go on stage.

My mother watched from the dining room window as I went to and from the cinema. She told me later that she could always tell what films I had seen when she saw me coming down the road. I might strut with squared shoulder and military bearing or sway in my saddle with an imaginary Stetson over my eyes as I trotted down the road beside Roy Rogers on Silver.

One Sunday afternoon in 1943 my parents went to hear Richard Tauber, a well-known tenor, Marion Nowoskowski, a

Polish bass and a Russian woman pianist in concert at the cinema – fund raising for the Red Cross. It was clearly a treat for them because my father said in his diary:

> It was for us both our first experience of such a concert and class of music but I hope not the last. The audience was very appreciative and both singers were called for encores.

And they kept the programme ever after.

I was tacitly considered too young for the treat. I said nothing but - wrote my father:

> Jan wanted to come with us at the last moment. We did not think she had any idea of coming until Florrie found a note in the pocket of her coat. No doubt she had been thinking and, not able to say anything, she wrote her thoughts: "Well, I wanted to come with you." Poor kid she was rather upset for a short while but after we had explained to her that it was hardly suitable for her and anyway our seats were booked, she took it as she always does, and no more was said.

What a conformable child! Or was my note a way of instilling parental guilt?

During the war there was little time for Mog to see old friends or make new ones. One who did come into our lives was Nancy B. [Bennett], the lady who slept in the dugout with us. Bee lived in one of the Gracemead Cottages almost opposite from our shop across Dog Kennel Lane. She was unmarried and had retired to Hatfield to live with and keep house for her brother. Bee had a nutcracker of a face: large tortoiseshell rimmed glasses perched on a slightly hooked nose and an upturned pointed chin which could have connected her in my mind with a witch but she was jolly, companionable and full of stories. She was perhaps nearer my grandmother in age but very friendly with Mog and would accompany them both to flower shows and shops, invite us for tea and always for a glass of sherry at the New Year served in delicate Victorian glasses which she eventually gave to Mog along with her own recipe book.

I still have the book, its cover stained and its pages ragged and brown at the edges. Some of the recipes were those used by Bee when she cooked at a hotel in Grantham and are recorded in her flowing hand. Most of the recipes are somewhat dated, the desserts requiring too many packet jellies and condensed milk – like that for Jellied Fig pudding and Marrow Cream but we have used her recipe for Orange marmalade with success. One section is grandly entitled "M. Avignons of the Ritz Hotel" with his recipes for Christmas pudding and celebratory cakes. Then a section for homemade wines: clover, beetroot, marigold and cowslip amongst the more conventional ingredients and hosts of recipes for gingerbread and biscuits. The book concludes triumphantly with a proven recipe for cough mixture and a somewhat dubious recipe consisting of peppermint oil, aniseed, cloves, paregoric, burnt sugar, honey and guaicum. Since the last was used centuries ago as a cure for syphilis, I wonder about that one, though to be fair it was probably another cough syrup. Bee's Chocolate soufflé has remained a winner, though an electric mixer has cut the beating time and we do not fancy cherries as a decoration.

4 eggs,   4oz caster sugar
½ pint milk   ¼ lb chocolate powder
5 leaves of gelatine

Beat the whites of the eggs very stiffly. Then beat the yolks and sugar together for ten minutes. Melt the gelatine and chocolate powder in the milk over a very slow heat not allowing it to get very warm or it will curdle when dissolved. Stir the mixture into the egg mix with a spoon and mix well. When it is beginning to set, stir in the stiff whites. Mix well and pour into a glass dish. When set, decorate with cream (whipped but not too stiff) and cherries.

On the rare occasions when Mog and Gran Hope went out together I would be invited to tea with Bee. We would sit in the dark little parlour, the table covered with a starched white cloth over a green velour cover. A tea tray would appear and a plate of homemade biscuits – an economical recipe which could be sometimes be spirited out of the rations. I felt quite grown up helping to toast bread over a bright coal fire burning in the black leaded grate. On the mantelpiece stood two silver framed photographs: one of a small boy, the other of a young man in naval uniform - a smart, good looking young chap with a suspicion of a hooked nose. Both were of Jock, who Bee said was her sister's son. During the war he was killed at sea. His death affected her powerfully and she was extremely sad for months. My mother told me later that she suspected that Jock was really her illegitimate child who, to preserve the proprieties, had been quietly taken under the wing of her sister. If so, how sad that she was unable to grieve openly.

Having presumably retired from catering and requiring some income Bee presided over a tiny shop at the end of Dog Kennel Lane at the beginning of the footpath which led through the allotments to the Council Estate at Dellfield. The shop was just a shed belonging to Charlie Moore, the tobacconist in St Albans Road. It was seemingly held together by the brightly coloured metal advertising signs attached to the lapped wood sides. I remember the shop for the sweets but she also sold a few cheap magazines, tobacco and some basic groceries, for the signs shouted their wares. Inside there was a dark wooden counter behind which Nancy served and, lining the back wall, rows of narrow shelves were divided by wooden turned supports. The shop was strategically placed as there was a path beside it that led to Newtown primary school in a housing estate called Dellfield, so many children passed by and their fathers went to and from work.

My visits to the shop must have started before the war and I remember the 1½d Sherbet dabs in yellow cardboard tubes from which I sucked the delicious lemon powder but indulged in them less frequently once rationing began. Liquorice was, I believe, unrationed but not so appealing. Before such privation Mog and I would visit the shop buying provisions of barley sugar or peppermints in small paper bags before going for a walk through the allotments to Roe Green. Vegetable growing was, of course, a serious business and the rows of neat allotments bordered by narrow grass paths were fun to run around. One allotment belonging to Mr. Doggett housed a brick built sty. Mog and I would walk towards it chanting "Pig,pig, pig,pig!" so that the occupants would come out of their house and Mog would lift me up to see the two young pigs rooting around the vegetable peelings in their trough. When I could reach I would scratch the coarse hair on the backs and they would look up snuffling appreciatively, their damp snouts rubbing against my arms. What could be spared from peelings from our vegetables and other left overs cooked into a smelly mash for our chickens were passed to Mr. Doggett for the pigs.

Another short walk was taken usually with my grandmother. Up the Right of way opposite and out on to Stockbreach Common. Not exciting? Ah, but you should know that Mrs. Moore whose husband Charlie had taken over our first shop, kept her Persian cats on the Common in a large shed with a wire run to allow them exercise. Gran and I would stop for a long time while I tried to entice the superior snub nosed

Persians to come to the wire to be tentatively stroked with a finger through the wire. "You watch out," said Gran. "They may bite you," but mostly they sat on their shelves or in baskets supremely indifferent to my lures. They were valuable pedigree creatures but there was no thought that they might be stolen.

A walk in the afternoon was almost a ritual. At first I would be taken in a push chair – perhaps to Old Hatfield where there was shopping to be done. When we reached the quiet little spinney in front of Lothair Villas that separated Cranborne Road from the railway I was allowed to walk and would climb the steps of the girder passenger bridge which had an open network of iron struts. I would listen with excited anticipation in case there was an approaching express train. Then I would run forward to stand above the rail where the train would whoosh beneath me with a tremendous roar. Terrified but thrilled I could see the sparks and the bright glow of the fire in the boiler and be enveloped in the steam and the sooty smell.

As I grew older walks were more varied. If my mother had the time she, like my Dad, would walk with me in Hatfield Park, trap beaver in the Canadian North West, follow a trail, or help me to climb trees. On one occasion I, having climbed over the bole of a tree could not get down. After encouragement and advice failed she went off to fetch a ladder she had seen leaning against a haystack and lugged it back, only to find I had gathered up my small courage and jumped. On fine summer afternoons we would take our tea up the park. She and Gran Hope would sit and talk or knit while I climbed over a huge fallen oak tree, known by many Hatfield children as The Ship. And sometimes she would join me and we would be pirates on the rolling main.

The Park of course, belonged to the Salisbury family. We always went "Up" the park, never "down" or "to". Did that give it the same status as London to which we always went "Up" though it was seventeen miles south of Hatfield? It was our own piece of wilderness, playground, snow runs, somewhere to watch cricket, find conkers, catch tiddlers, sail toy yachts and it was free to residents of the town.

It was also a place of family stories. To enter we went through the ornate iron gates past the Station Lodge where my father's uncle had to use the front door for three months because he had set fire to a tree when his father was lodge keeper. Walking over the viaduct that ran high above Park Street Pop would point out the cottage chimneys below into which he and his friends would try to lob stones. On the first piece of grass after the viaduct was the brooding iron lump of a First World War tank. It was in the park that the prototype tanks were tried out in 1916.

One summer holiday Greta and I were dared by two boys we knew to climb up into the tank. We scrambled with difficulty up onto the caterpillar tracks, edged our way to the entrance and dropped inside. It was smelly, rusty, damp, and soggy with dead leaves and fag ends, the latter no doubt left by illicit young smokers. I think I had hoped to get some sense of being a tank driver but "Let's get out," said Greta. "It stinks." Getting out was more difficult. Luckily there was an old wooden box inside which doubtless others had used as a step.

When young I was taken up the Park first in a pram, then a pushchair. Mog washed up Sunday lunch while my Dad went off to watch the cricket and she would follow with me. The cricket ground was below the North front of the house, with a road and bushes on one side and bounded by a fine avenue of graceful lime trees on the other. There my father would be seated on a rug chatting with friends. When of an age to enjoy the cricket myself I would go with him. The cricket was leisurely, the clapping gentle, little excitement: the best of spectator sports.

Once Dad and I took my small toy yacht in hand and walked to a stream towards the Mill green gate. There the little red hull with white sail bobbed about on the water frequently catching in the tree roots that spilled into the stream. Longer walks would take us up Queen Elizabeth's Avenue to the gnarled old trunk hooped with iron bands said to be the tree under or upon which Princess Elizabeth was seated when she was told that her sister Mary was dead and she was Queen. The trunk was so old and dead it was difficult to imagine the scene. Old Mrs. Maddocks, the chief gamekeeper's wife, who lived beyond the Oak, when asked once if she was not frightened going home in the dark after Women's Institute, replied "Oh no, you see the lady in white always walks with me." Dad and I would turn left at the Oak and walk to the Broadwater, where the River Lea had been widened to make slow moving calm stretch of water. On the far side was the Vineyard, in my childhood quite neglected, but its rosy red brick walls built in 1633 had an air of forlorn grandeur.

But it was more often my mother that walked in the park with me. We would marvel at the old oak tree, its grey scarred trunk wound like an elephant and curled at the tip, giving its name to Elephant dell down which we would scramble into a sea of bracken. Many of the trees were ancient and had large swollen boles on their sides. One spring day Greta and I, aged about eight went for a walk in the park and, greedy for some of the myriads of wild daffodils, we picked a bunch each – something we knew was forbidden. Horror! We heard voices. Swiftly we hid the daffodils in the base of a hollow tree and walked out to the path. Coming up it were the tall, gaunt and dignified figures of Lord and Lady Salisbury[42]. Quiet and kindly, they made polite conversation with us, asking our names and enquiring if we were enjoying our walk. We replied politely and they passed on their way. We felt guilty, but not such miserable offenders that we failed to pick up our flowers before trotting home.

---

[42] The 4th Marquess of Salisbury

One more dangerous escapade I dimly remember. There was a lake to the east of Hatfield house in a private part of the grounds. The boat house contained little but an old dilapidated rowing boat. Greta and I having found a way to a path by the lake climbed into the boat and sat there, dreaming of rowing away to far distant lands.

When snow clothed the slopes many children would set out for the park dragging sledges or carrying tin trays for tobogganing. My sledge was a heavy wooden affair made by one of our assistants. The metal runners torn from the sides of tea chests soon rusted. Why do I remember still with chagrin that two boys told me that my sledge was ruining the hard smooth surface of the sledging slope for they could see the rust marks? Of course it didn't. We would play until long after our hands and feet were frozen, then walk home dragging the sledges and shaking our hands as our fingers thawed and we felt excruciating "hot-ache." Gran Hope fussed: "I've put your slippers to warm", she said, "You'll get chilblains."

One late summer's day in the park with a picnic was my parents' annual holiday during the war. We would pack baskets with flasks of tea, paste sandwiches, homemade cake and the first ripe apples. We would walk as far as we could, my parents breasting the bracken which almost came over my head; find convenient logs and sit in the sun. Mog and Pop no doubt revelled in the peace and the absence of noise and business.

Blackberries must have ripened later than they do now for it was the week before I returned to school in the third week of September that Gran Hope, in a hat bedecked with felt flowers, my mother and I set out to pick blackberries. How did Mog know where the best fruits were? I believe they were in a private part of the park called Coombe Wood. There was a notice saying: 'Private' but we would walk over to the far edge of the wood on the summer-dried crisp turf, sprinkled with rabbit droppings, avoiding the many mole hills and, since there was no notice there, I presume Mog thought it fair game. The comforting memories of childhood: the blackberries hung in ropes on the brambles, baskets grew heavy and my mouth was soon purple. Hard boiled eggs and bread and butter with a flask of tea made a lunch and then we would trek back, tired and prickly, stopping by at Gran Tingey's to leave her some fruit then home to make blackberry and apple jam, blackberry jelly and perhaps a sumptuous juicy pie for supper. I don't think my mother bottled fruit and we had no refrigerator so the fruit had to be used quickly.

Short walks in the Park would be in at the Station gate and back via The Old Palace. I loved the rosy red Tudor bricks of the building, the cool arches, old roses spread eagled against the walls. "That's where Gran Tingey was born," said my mother, pointing up to a room above the lodge arch. Then into Fore street, where the houses tumbled down the steep hill to the Eight Bells at the bottom.

It was later when I was in my teens that my cousin Diana and I rode ponies in the park. Diana had one of her own and I used to exercise a fat little pony for the estate manager's daughter who was at boarding school. We would take long rides up to Milwards Park and round the edge of the park towards Essendon, for whole days of quiet plodding.

I have already brought Gran Hope in to the scene. She was always there, gentle and ready to help. What of my other grandparents? Their home, where they had moved when my parents were married, was referred to by us all as "55" and it was further to the east in St Albans Road. It was a house which the architect Dudley Ward designed for them and which won a prize in Country Life in 1936 as the best small suburban house of the year. It was a surprising thing for my grandfather to do. I wonder how it happened. By then my grandmother was a semi-invalid so he probably felt it would be more comfortable for her than a first-floor flat. It was detached, built of red brick in the neo- Georgian style with a gently pitched roof and wide eaves. It was light inside with plenty of sash windows. There was a garage on the side attached to the house by a linking coal shed. All the woodwork was of natural pine. We three girls liked the staircase which occupied the centre of the house and provided a balcony for us to act plays.

The kitchen was rectangular with a window overlooking the back garden. On one side there was a wall of cupboards with polished pine door and on the other a coke-fired boiler and a cooker in a tiled recess. Besides the large wooden table and chairs there was one more comfortable chair with cushions which was mostly occupied by Tibby the cat. The sink and draining board with a wooden plate rack to the side and work top beneath was up one step in virtually an alcove at the front. There was hardly room for more than one person to wash up or prepare vegetables. There was also a walk in pantry with slate shelves and a red tiled floor.

The dining room was at the back behind the hall, not a large room but with two long sash windows and a hatch connecting it with the kitchen. The sitting room ran from front to the back of the house with a French door opening on the side and a window at either end. One wall was dominated by a fine oil painting of a 19th century Swiss mountain scene. Grandad enjoyed going to auctions or to his brother's shop and bought good pieces of furniture and pictures.

Upstairs were three bedrooms. Joan and Norman were then unmarried and lived at home before the war. Joan kept several Film Lovers' Annuals with glamorous pictures of Stars on the cover. I enjoyed looking at them when I stayed in her bedroom when she was away in the A.T.S. The bathroom was next to her room and there was a separate lavatory on each floor.

The back garden was large and divided into two by a tall trellis fence. There were flower beds near the back of the house, and more up each side of the large lawn, in the middle of which was a huge Sycamore tree surrounded by lavender bushes. The fruit and vegetable garden was behind the trellis and there we would enjoy tasting the raspberries and strawberries and helping ourselves to apple and pears in season. Beside the garden was a field used by Hollier's horses that pulled the milk carts. On the other was the path leading to the "Rec" an oval patch of grass big enough to play football and a desultory collection of playground swings and roundabouts. Nowadays there are other houses on either side and the kitchen garden must have been sold as a building plot. When I was small 55 felt as if it were in the country. It was, I suppose, about half a mile from our shop and I used to walk there unaccompanied from an early age.

Gran Tingey was quiet, tall and slightly austere. She had had a serious operation in her early forties, probably bowel cancer, and had a colostomy bag for the rest of her life. She was not cuddly or comforting but a matriarch. The family was her life. She had us frequently to tea and would have her grandchildren in turn sometimes to stay at weekends, kindly doing it to give the parents a break. What do I really remember of her when I was a child? She never read stories to me, although my cousin, who is twenty years younger than I, remembers being told stories by her when she stayed with her parents. She would let me help her prepare vegetables for dinner and we would pick at bits of raw cauliflower for which we both had a liking. "We better not have any more or there will be none left." She herself ate little and I noticed in later years that she seemed to live on little but cream crackers. Management of her colostomy must always have been difficult especially in the early years when the appliances were primitive and her bedroom smelled faintly of faeces and disinfectant though she was scrupulously clean I remember care but little laughter. She came into her own at Christmas but that is another story to be told.

And as for Grandad: he was a bluff, genial man who told a good joke and, according to his children, loved poetry. When they returned from school he would often ask them, "Have you learned any poetry today?" He was perhaps happiest walking in the country round Hatfield of an evening or, even more, sitting in the White Lion with a pint of mild and bitter. I was told that when any soldier came into the pub Grandad would shake his hand and leave half a crown in the man's palm. He smoked Nut Brown tobacco. It had a thick pungent smell that hung about him and permeated the house. He did not enjoy having a bath and when on infrequent occasions he did so, Grandma would say "I must put the flags out". He was not particularly active in the community like his father, or like his brother Tom who was on the Council and a J.P. but he was liked. The Gypsy Smiths who went travelling in the summer used to stop their caravans outside the shop and leave their Lemsford Road deeds with him for safe keeping. He used also to keep a store of cash to change £5 notes for the railway workers who lived in Gracemead.

One of my earliest memories is sitting on his lap when he had returned from the shop. "I don't like your whickers" I said, stroking his moustache with a stubby finger. Gran Tingey would have a plate of marmite sandwiches ready for him, the crusts neatly removed and he would pop little pieces into my mouth. Each grandchild was initiated into Marmite in the same way. Once Tibby, their cat walked past and turned away from us, his tail high in the air. "What's that Grandad?" I asked pointing. "That's his little sixpence," came the answer.

I don't think Grandad ever complained or moaned about having an invalid wife nor do I think he ever strayed into another bed. He worked hard and well at the shop, chivvying and teasing the assistants. Like his wife he enjoyed having his family about him. Sadly he and my mother were not on entirely easy terms. I believe he considered my mother slightly prudish and that it was she who stopped my father from joining him in the pub. In fact, beer made my father sick and he did not enjoy that easy fraternity. I do wish that one could have the dead back occasionally. I am sure that Grandad and our younger daughter would have delighted in each other's company, sharing a drink and exchanging tall stories.

On Sunday evenings he and my father would take a walk around the lanes and I often went with them. We would set out at a good pace, Grandad swinging his thick walking stick with a carved dog's head on the handle, which had belonged to his father. Up the lanes we would stride, the hawthorn heavy with scented may blossom and the hedges fizzy with cow parsley. At harvest time I would be dwarfed by the wheat or barley for in those days the stalks were tall and the ears waved above my head. Sometimes we would walk over the fields to Mr. White's farm. There I would amuse myself looking at the pigs while Grandad talked farming and weather with his crony and my father would listen, chipping in the odd word. On a walk round the lanes in March 1943 my father was reflective in his diary:

> Birds were singing everywhere, mostly thrushes. The hedges and fields are fast coming to life and blackthorn is in blossom in the more sheltered spots. All this in peacetime brings joy, reminding one of long sunny days, of flowers, fruit and the smell of hay new cut, but in war the expectancy of spring reminds one of gathering evil.

We are expecting, waiting for something to happen and know it will be horror and suffering for many but know that unless that something does happen we shall not be able to greet future springs with full joy.

My world was small, domestic and cosy. We did not go far and distance was confined by the amount we could walk, then cycle. Excursions by bus and train were rare events. Yet Mog also took me to London during the war once or twice more than the memorable trip to the theatre. We would walk the streets seeing men in uniform with kitbags and tin hats. The treat would be tea at the Lyons Corner House in the Strand. We would walk into a fug of smoke, tea and a chatter of voices. Mog would have a pot of tea and I had a glass of hot lemonade in a metal holder – such sophistication. Visits to the cinema were not confined to Hatfield. Holiday visits to St Albans meant that we saw such varied delights as *George Formby, Jane Eyre, Buffalo Bill and the Arabian Nights.* And on one day before going to the cinema we went to Verulamium to see the museum and the Roman remains and Mog enjoyed telling me about her visit to the archaeological excavations when she was a girl.

Almost all that I have described happened while war raged in Europe and the Far East. Looked at from seventy years on it still seems quietly idyllic. Children of today would find it dull. It was slow moving, ambling, unrushed and in retrospect, endless sunny days punctuated by snowy winters. The only significant interruption to my day dreaming and pretend games was not the war but school.

Chapter 10

School

"Good observation, Tingey!" were treasured words of praise from Miss Norman at Goldings where my brother first went to school in 1951. It became a family saying. My parents wanted to send me there ten years earlier. Goldings was a real Dame School held in a large well-built wooden cabin in the garden. Ada Norman was a renowned teacher and an enthusiast for open-air activity, so that the doors and the windows of the classrooms at Goldings were rarely closed. She believed in allowing her charges to choose their activities and encouraged originality. It would have been a good choice.

Unfortunately Goldings was full in 1941, so their second choice was Newtown House, which had the advantage of being near to us in St Albans Road. It was a small private school in a gaunt building of three storeys plus a half-basement and had two rows of chimneys at either end. Its only distinguished feature was the white stone porch with steps up to the front door, flanked by wide stone balustrades. There was a gravel drive at the front and one side, with a large grassed area edged and studded by trees. Miss Mary Thomas and Miss Joan Burrows who owned Alexandra House, the little private school attended by my Aunt Joan, moved to Newtown House around 1934. Mog took me for an interview in the summer of 1941. We were taken into a sitting room on the left side of the hall on the ground floor. Miss Thomas had white hair piled artistically on top of her head, wore a black dress and was small and spritely.

On the first day of the autumn term, wearing the brown blazer with a yellow badge that was part of the uniform, I walked with my mother up the steps to the front door – steep steps for short legs – and was put in the Transition class. This was in a high-ceilinged room on the ground floor. The class teacher was Miss Burrows. That day I was given my first reading card. I could write my name and knew some number before I went to the school but had not properly learned to read. The card was on thick soft card, almost like blotting paper and had a small line drawing in yellow and brown at the top. It concerned Rover the dog and two boring children called Dick and Dora. 'Give Rover the ball. Rover has the ball.' I must have been close to reading because I remember nothing more about the process.

My first school report, lovingly kept by my mother said that I had "made a very good beginning, and was a keen little worker." Perhaps then, but not always. Our exercise books were half sized and thin. It was wartime, after all. Looking at one of my exercise books kept by my mother I am struck by the dullness of it all. Much time was spent on spelling, dictation and handwriting, painstakingly inscribing words between the narrow lines with many rubbings out and overwriting. Not much encouragement to be creative.

In the September term of 1942 I moved upstairs to the next class. The classroom had probably been a main bedroom and had a window to the front of the house. There was a fireplace with an over mantel that was half hidden by a large blackboard on an easel, and a wardrobe which held books and stationery. The ledges of the doors and the tops of the cupboards either side of the fireplace were dusty with chalk. The iron framed desks with a hard and unyielding bench incorporated into them, seated two and there was only a shelf below the desktop. The desktops were ridged and gouged by destructive predecessors. Small china inkwells fitted into the top of the desk beside a groove for pens and pencils.

This class was taught by a Miss Tarrant, a tall young woman with her hair in a bun and a cheerful manner. The only book in multiple copies was Kingsley's The Water Babies. We read from it, copied passages for handwriting and used it for

dictation. Not surprisingly I've never read it since – though it did give me sympathy for little chimney sweeps. We appear to have had but one exercise book so the Water Babies rubbed shoulders with occasional bits of Grammar, half pages of nature:
The mistletoe is a Parerisite
The Holly is an evergreen with prickling leaves to protect the tree for some animals like the leaves.[43]

some geography and history:
The warrior queen's name was Boadicea. Her husband was King of Norfolk and Suffolk. He left half his wealth to the Roman Emperor, hoping he would protect his wife and daughters, but the Emperor seized all the estate and ill-treated the women.

Then back to The Water Babies.
I went home for lunch, but my cousins, who were also pupils, stayed. Goodness knows what they had to eat. Sometimes I would go back early to play and on wet days, apparently unsupervised, we would nip down to the damp, dark basement and take turns to haul each other up in the dumb waiter which went from the basement to the first floor. It was a dark, dusty cupboard and creaked dangerously as one slowly ascended. I suspect I avoided taking my turn as often as possible for I was too timid. We also played Tom Tiddler's Ground[44], Chase and Hide and Seek among the trees. On sport's day I actually won a race – Egg and Spoon. Mog remembered

---

[43] In fact Holly was used as a supplement or replacement for hay when food was in short supply or the land covered with snow so the animals could not graze.
[44] Tom Tiddler's Ground, is an ancient children's game in which one player, "Tom Tiddler," stands on a heap of stones, gravel, etc.; other players rush onto the heap, crying "Here I am on Tom Tiddler's ground while other children try to invade his property. – Wikipedia 2016

me standing quietly under a tree after the event hugging the glory of it to myself.

I remember few of the other pupils in detail, though I do recall Elsie Epps – or truthfully, recall where she lived. I can hardly picture her in school but her home was at the top of the Second Right of Way, a pretty cottage with a garden at the front and it had a well which contained clear, sweet water. Then there was a lad with very dark hair and a tanned skin. Some of the parents thought he was from a gypsy family. Prejudice flared when my mother and others discovered lice in their children's hair. They presumed we had caught them from this boy. She told me after, however, that she found that one of our shop staff had them and it was probably I who had taken them into the school. I am not sure that she had the courage to confess.

My time at Newtown House was short for in January 1944 Miss Thomas died and the school closed. There was a sale of her possessions and my mother bought for me a pair of bookends- seated man and woman in eighteenth century costume, now long gone and for herself she bought a pair of Edwardian youngsters dressed in white with yellow trim holding tennis racquets and balls. They still stand on a windowsill ready to start a game.

So what to do with me then? I remember no discussion. Perhaps I was not consulted at first. I suspect it was my mother who suggested that my father wrote to St Albans High School for Girls, an independent Church school. One of her childhood friends had been there and Mog had envied her though there was no way her mother could have afforded the fees. Also a certain Florence Marjorie Robertson had been a pupil some years before, and Anna Neagle, for that was her stage name, was one of my mother's favourite actresses. Mog probably also considered that as they took girls from four years old to eighteen I would not have to change schools again. The school had moved from Holywell Hill in 1908 to what must have seemed a fine modern building at the northern end of St Albans which she would have passed frequently when delivering dresses from Sparys to customers living in the large Edwardian houses nearby. Several of these had been bought by the school for use as boarding houses.

Securing a place for me was somewhat protracted. My father noted in his diary

> 28th February, 1944: Today I have written to St Albans High School regarding Janet's schooling. In these days of raids one feels that tomorrow is only maybe and that life is so uncertain. Of course, this is always the case and things can't be stopped on account of uncertainty.

A week later he reported that my mother and I had been over to the school to see the headmistress and it was arranged that I would go for a test the following week. In the meantime, Pop tested me on my multiplication tables. On the morning my mother dressed me up in winter coat and Fair Isle beret and I sensed it was something of an occasion. Two teachers interviewed us in a room dominated by tall bookshelves and a large, dusty office desk. "What books have you read recently?" asked a tweed clad, grey haired lady with a cheery smile and thin legs? I thought hard. "I like Harper Cory's Wild Life Ways" I replied, "It is very interesting".

"What do you mean by interesting?" asked an even older lady with a bun. "Well, it is all about beaver and how they build lodges and dam streams."

The next question was "How many sixpences in half a crown? Followed by what are eleven twelves?" And that was it. So far so good, but Newtown House closed on 1st April and nothing was heard from the High School until the end of the month when we had a letter giving me a place and suggesting that we went to the school outfitters for the uniform.

Off we went to Plumbs, a shop in the London Road which was the official school outfitters. I imagine my mother may have been somewhat concerned about the cost and the clothing coupons required but I found the experience exciting. By then I had been reading school stories and being "kitted out" for school was all part of the ritual. The Junior school pupils wore saxe blue tweed skirts with a pinafore top and white Viyella blouse. A house tie was added on one's first day at the school. Thick navy blue knickers which doubled as gym-wear, a blue tweed overcoat and blue felt hat completed the winter uniform. By then I had graduated from wearing a Liberty bodice – a thick, fleecy sleeveless under garment which belied its name – but even then, winter clothes though warm were stiff and uncomfortable. But most of the winter uniform had to wait until September. Summer uniform, donned at the beginning of the summer term, consisted of a cotton dress, panama hat and the distinctive navy and yellow striped blazer – a larger version of which still resides in our dressing-up box. I suspect that the dresses were varied, though they had to be blue and white in pattern, depending on what material could be found and that my mother would have made mine herself.

By the 1st May my parents still did not know when I was to start. Mog, always pro-active, took me over to enquire but could not get a definite answer. My father was persuaded to phone the school that evening and I was to go next day.

Tuesday 2nd: No trouble getting Jan up this morning. At 7 o/c she was up and preparing to catch her bus at 8.20am. I must say she looked very nice and fresh in her outfit."

Sensibly the school started term on a Thursday and for the morning only when all that was done was settling girls into their classrooms, letting them organise their desks, then having a House meeting. On Friday, timetables, textbooks etc. were issued and any other administrative details sorted so that work started properly on a Monday.

My parents had not been told about the half-day and I realised that I had the whole afternoon to myself. Excited by this unexpected freedom I decided to visit Miss Spary who lived near to the school. I don't know what she thought about it but she gave me a drink and sent me on my way. I then decided to walk the five miles home to Hatfield rather than catch the 341 bus. I knew the way because Mog and I had explored the roads near to the school. I threaded the streets down to the Hatfield Road and along to Fleetville, a walk of under two miles but an adventure. The route was one I knew well, not so much because my grandmother had lived there, but we often travelled between the two towns on the bus. I passed the cemetery and the Ballito stocking factory and paused to look in the shop windows. I had only my 3d bus fare in my pocket and no coupons so I couldn't buy any sweets. When I reached Arthur Road I stopped and looked down the length of it feeling, I suspect, a certain reassurance for it was familiar ground. I grew tired before I reached Hatfield and caught a bus for the last two miles, arriving about the right time.

My father's comment in his diary that night was merely: "Jan arrived home at about 4.30. Little did we know that she had spent the afternoon partly at Miss Spary's and partly walking down to Fleetville before catching the bus. Like a young animal free for the first time to wonder and wander. She told us that the conductress said "Upstairs" but she said "Upstairs makes me not well" and the prompt answer was "Come inside then"'. Clearly my parents were not worried that their eight year old had been roaming the streets alone.

What do I remember of school in the last year of the war? The House meeting on the first day was daunting. I was told that I was to be in Julian House.[45] We were sent to a classroom and sitting on the floor in the front while older girls stood or perched on desks, we waited silently for our formidable housemistress, Miss Leather. She urged us to work hard to get house points, handed out red ties and house badges to we new girls.

My classroom, large and airy, was above the dining room and was sometimes taught by Miss Lee, the second mistress. What were we taught? I remember nothing other than occasionally being read stories of Robin Hood and drawing a map of the coalfields of Britain. I enjoyed neatly lining the coastline with blue crayon to represent the sea. School dinners were awful. It must have been hard to provide them in war time but fatty greasy meat and thin gravy followed by sponge pudding dripped with watered down syrup, did not appeal and we were not allowed to leave a scrap on our plates. Regular lectures from Miss Archibald, the Headmistress, at Assembly about not wasting food while poor starving children abroad needed it only got the subversive mutter of "Why don't you send it to them?" I once took the fatty gristly remains of meat home, wrapped in my hanky, displayed it on the kitchen table and said disgustedly: "There, that's what we are supposed to eat."

I did not enjoy playtime at first. I was still something of a loner and it took time for me to enjoying playing with others. Skipping was popular but I was hopeless. Despite Gran and Mog spending patient hours turning a rope for me I never got the hang of it. It must have been a disappointment to my mother who was an adept. Hopscotch, played by marking out the gritty, clinker path below the gym was marshalled by some girls who

---

[45] The four houses were all named after famous people of St Albans: Julian for Dame Juliana Berners, an abbess, Mandeville for the great traveller, Sir John Mandeville, Paris for Matthew of that name, a monk of the Abbey and Verulam after Francis Bacon, Lord Verulam

took a delight in criticising one's play and there was I think some verbal bullying which for a while spoiled the experience of school that in general I liked. It was then that the early experience of bilious attacks which had bedevilled some of my early years came in handy. I would occasionally feign sickness to enjoy a day off school – a morning when I could happily listen to Schools programmes on the radio, thoroughly enjoying 'How Things began' while trying to look wan and sickly. Sometimes it worked. On other occasions I was persuaded to go and would disconsolately pick up my satchel and droop down the stairs to catch the bus. Mog told me that feeling mean and hard hearted so she would catch the bus to St Albans to meet her ailing daughter only to see me skip out of school laughing with my friends.

The large asphalt playground surrounded on all sides by the main school, wooden hutted laboratories and the gym was the usual place of recreation in the morning break. One teacher would be on duty. I think now with guilt and sympathy of a tall young woman who had straight bobbed hair, wore a fawn tweed suit and sensible brogue shoes and was a source of entertainment. She must have taught classics because some of the older girls would beg her to spout Latin verse which she, guilelessly taking it for scholarly interest, would do at length and the perpetrators would nod seriously and then giggle into their hands. She had a habit of walking up and down the playground – sometimes continuing to recite but always rubbing her hand together and taking long mannish steps. Small girls would line up behind her and there would be a long trail of striding juniors rubbing their hands with wicked glee. Did she never guess? Did she realise she was being made fun of but not being able to stop it so miserably accepted herself as a laughing stock? Girls can be cruel. Did I join in? I don't remember but I fear so.

At lunch time we had to line up outside the dining room

and members of our class would fight to stand next to Brenda Raven, a popular child with plaits. I don't think she was particularly remarkable but she had a great following. At first I was beneath notice but we did become friends and I was even asked to stay with her for the weekend in Wheathampstead. It was something of a disaster. We shared a bed – a feather bed which I had not experienced before and found suffocatingly warm. Perhaps that was why I was so miserable and homesick that my parents had to come to fetch me home after only one night.

After school lunch we juniors had a rest period. We had to lie in rows upon the floor of the hall for – perhaps half an hour. Was this only when it was raining? My inventive father made me a tiny Cat's whisker radio in a matchbox to which I would surreptitiously listen. The crackling voices were at least an antidote to the boredom. Mog sometimes provided me with a small tin containing a small amount of cocoa powder and sugar into which I could dip my finger – a concoction which she had herself had as a child. Other illicit delights were spinning buttons on cotton with resulting hum and playing surreptitiously with homemade paper fortune tellers. All this depended on the craze of the moment.

I have a plethora of odd memories. Miss Archibald was 63 when I entered the school in 1944 and had been head since 1916. She retired in 1950. Despite her superior height, she had something of the air of Queen Victoria, her white hair scraped back into a bun over which, most of the time, she wore a battered black felt hat. Her dark dresses were covered by her long academic gown which was dusty and covered with hairs of the scruffy little Cairn terrier who accompanied her everywhere. I remember being fascinated when, upon her birthday, one of the sixth form girls – mighty and beyond the aura of we little ones - gave her a short oration in Latin which no doubt was well rehearsed and practiced. Miss Archibald replied extempore in

Greek. She had been a Greek scholar which accounted for the visits of her friend Professor Gilbert Murray to the school, and why the older girls performed his translation of a Greek play every year. I don't recall the one I saw in my first year, though I think it was a tragedy. Indeed the only one which remains a vivid impression was probably towards the end of my time at the school. It was *The Frogs* by Aristophanes when a chorus of frogs provided by juniors sat hunched by the side of the stage croaking "Brekekekèx-koàx-koáx" and I cherish still the memory of Heracles, played by the buxom school cricket captain, her physique developed by years of cricket and lacrosse, garbed in a leopard skin and wielding a club.

In my first two years the school still produced Tableaux Vivant. Wikipedia states "the most recent heyday of the tableau vivant was the 19th century, with virtually nude tableaux vivants or poses plastiques providing a form of erotic entertainment." Believe me, ours were not like that! A large gilt picture frame was put up on the stage and behind the curtains a girl dressed as – say Gainsborough's Blue Boy, or several girls making an eighteenth century group painting would be carefully shifted into the correct position. Then the curtains would open, soft music would be played and the audience – which usually included parents and school governors – would applaud. I was mystified by it.

Miss Archibald, besides her administrative duties, taught Greek, which I wanted to learn when we had to choose our classical subject at twelve, but not being lucky enough to be either a Scot or a clergyman's daughter I was put into the Latin set. She also, along with Miss Lee taught Divinity.[46] Teaching was hardly the word. More often than not she would sweep into our classroom where we sat dutifully silent, order: "Learn the Collect for the second Sunday after Trinity" and sweep out

---

[46] As John Morrish once wrote in The Tablet "Well, it was that kind of school and it was a long time ago."

again. I doubt if we were even tested on it. She found it difficult to relate to her pupils, rarely knowing our names and usually a somewhat peremptory "You!" was an indication that she wished to speak to one of us.

Not all the teaching was poor, but in that last year of the war there were severe restrictions on materials. Exercise books were thin and mean and we were abjured not to waste paper. Textbooks were old and second-hand. Indeed at the end of a year there would be a sale of books from one year group to another so there were torn pages, pencilled aids to learning and even mild graffiti. Unscrupulous seniors would try to pass on outdated textbooks as being essential for the next year's curriculum.

The desks were as battered as the books. Very few could be written on without a thick pad of paper beneath for they were scored and rutted and the inkwells were filled with thick gooey ink. One day when no teacher had arrived to take our lesson a bored girl dipped a small piece of blotting paper in her inkwell, drew it out on the nib of her pen and flicked it at the ceiling. A moment of madness obviously came over us and we all had a go. Soon a satisfying pattern of navy spots adorned the ceiling. I don't remember when this was noticed but letters were sent home and we all had to pay for the ceiling to be redecorated. Sensible. Otherwise the classrooms were dull and bare. Pictures on the walls were standard prints. How many of my generation have Millais' *The Boyhood of Raleigh,* Yeames, *When did you last see your father?* etched on our memories?

The corridors were wide and covered in parquet flooring; the stairs at either end were so shallow that one was tempted to run up two at a time. "No running" would come the stern voice of the prefect on duty, leaning for comfort on a lukewarm radiator. When a doodlebug raid occurred in the middle of the day we all sat cross-legged and leaned against the walls of the central corridor. There was a long shelter in the small field below the school but it was nearly always running with water.

Those members of staff that I remember up until the end of the war were spinsters, some of whom had lost their fiancés in WWI. I, of course, remember them as being very old but they were mostly in their late forties. They were devoted to their calling and determined to develop our characters as well as teach us our tables. There was Miss Meiklejohn – Mick - who was the games mistress, usually to be seen in a gymslip. She was enthusiastic and competent and expected dedication. I hated "Gym" because I was useless. Couldn't climb ropes, couldn't vault over the horse, couldn't hang upside down on the bars and high jump was beyond me. All I could do was balance steadily on the narrow rail of upturned forms. Once I reached puberty, believe me, I claimed to have my period at least every three weeks because we were allowed to sit out at such times.

However, though not a natural games player I was, in the first couple of years, good at cricket – only because I was keen. Not only had I absorbed the play in Hatfield Park, but I had been taken to Lord's when I was seven. My mother had come with us expecting to take me off to the Zoo when I was bored but I would have none of it. My father used to spend many evenings bowling to me in the garden and I was an early adherent before other girls had lifted a bat. My cricketing bible was the 1934 book: *Cricket for Women and Girls* by Marjorie Pollard; a doughty proponent of the women's game who played cricket and hockey for England in the thirties. She urged girls "to hit the ball with the enthusiasm of any village blacksmith". Once my classmates became more experienced my performance dwindled. In later years I never achieved the distinction of putting a ball through the window of the pavilion –for which the batsman was awarded half a crown by Mick and presumably not asked to pay for the glass.

We were also taught lacrosse. My mother advertised in the paper for a lacrosse stick and one was found for £1. New ones were very hard to come by. Before we were allowed to play a game we had to do 'stick work' which meant passing the ball one to another until we could catch it with some proficiency and then learn to dodge opposing players while cradling the ball in our sticks. I delighted in lacrosse as being a game originally played by American Indians and also having no boundaries. Netball and rounders were played as well but they did not excite me. To play all these games we had to walk for just under a mile in crocodile down Townsend Drive and through a wood to the school fields.

I had been learning the piano for a couple of years, taught by Miss Smith in Hatfield, the sister of Kipper Smith the fishmonger. I would walk down to Batterdale after school, my music in a smart leather case, sit in her dark little parlour and learn the notes, simple scales and such pieces as *The Moonlight march of the Gnomes* and *What do the Bells say*? When I went to the High School my parents thought it would be simpler if I took lessons there which was quite an expense at 2 ½ guineas a term. (The school fees then were 10guineas a term). As a result I came under the tutelage of Tan, Miss Tansy.

There was a character: large and slightly ungainly, she had fair hair, nicotined stained fingers and a loud cheery laugh. She was responsible for all the music in the school, played the viola herself in the somewhat ragged school orchestra, played the organ in St Albans Abbey when we went for services but also took piano pupils. She taught in a sliver of a room off the passage to the domestic science kitchen. It just held Tan on her chair and a piano with stool. The room was always stuffy with cigarette smoke and the pungent smell of Meggazone throat pastilles which she hoped vainly would disguise her habit. I was neither a conscientious nor a gifted pianist. "How is Janet getting on?" enquired my father at a meeting with Tan. "Well she can do well when she practises, but she'll never set the Thames on fire." Once my lack of practice brought such rebuke that I wept. "Look," said Tan, with firm kindness, if I was only teaching you music I should be doing only half my job. I want you to be conscientious and able to discipline yourself to do the right thing."

Tan was also the musical director of the annual nativity Pageant, a High School institution which had been started by Mademoiselle Dupy in 1921 and was performed annually until her retirement in 1939. It was revived in 1941 so I was privileged to participate in it for every year of my time at the school. It was phased out in the late sixties.

Nowadays it would be regarded as dated and simplistic, consisting of tableaux and different processions going up to adore the child in the stable with Joseph and Mary and angels grouped behind. My own rôles started, like so many other young pupils, in the children's procession. I suspect that only the fair, angelic looking little girls started as baby angels wearing wings built up with stiff white net. I was a Welsh girl in my first year. My mother had made most of the costume including a black shiny hat surmounting a frilly lace cap which she had made for a dancing display at home.

Another year I became a page to the three kings. Mick insisted that as we came away from the manger down the steps of the stage we were not to look down but keep our eyes fixed on the clock at the back of the hall. I do not suppose there would have been any sympathy if one had fallen down the steps, but of course, none of us did. (Rather like the insistence that one did not cough in prayers, it was a good discipline). I was two years in the "Sorrows" procession, first as a leper and then a beggar. I liked rôles which gave me an opportunity to get into the part!

I must have had an old face, wrinkled before my time, because I was selected as the "old king" three years running. I remember Sunday afternoon performances in St Albans Abbey and being made up artistically by Miss Leather, who bit her lip in her inimitable way as she concentrated on my face. Of course, I dared not move. She would use one of the medieval tombs as her workbench and there were neat rows of greasepaint and boxes of powder – grey for me – arranged around a recumbent stone knight

That was, of course after 1950, but from the beginning I remember Tan and Mick getting irritable and cross with each other and the crosser they grew the more polite they became. Looking back I realise they must have been tired. It was a mammoth task for it involved virtually every girl in the school. And the rehearsals took up many hours – no doubt somewhat resented by other members of staff and probably by some parents.

But the sum was greater than the parts; especially when we performed in the Abbey on a winter's afternoon, the Lady Chapel misty and darkening as the light faded. There was a sense of mysticism which outweighed conventional religion. The very familiarity of the music and the ritual brought a stability and sense of spirituality which has probably stayed with the performers, albeit unconsciously for the rest of their lives.

The school was affiliated to the Church of England so there were services at St. Albans Abbey once a term. They were not particularly inspiring but it was an accepted part of the rhythm of school life. I suspect there was an inbuilt snobbery in that other schools attended but the High School, I believe, always provided the lesson readers. In my later years I was trained to read and it has been a valuable asset since Mick would take us down for rehearsal and we had to make our voices carry without benefit of a P.A. system. "I can't hear you!" came Mick's authoritative voice from the back of the longest cathedral nave in Britain.

Other departures from the curriculum were few but regular. There was The Flower Show – a sort of miniature copy of those held in villages. There were classes for fresh flower arrangements, books of dried flowers and leaves, flower paintings. Much more interesting to me was the annual Pet Show. In my first year my father used one of the shop vans so that he and my mother could bring my cream guinea pig with black ears and nose to be shown. The previous evening I stood her on the kitchen table and brushed her fur until it shone and ensured that her nails were clean and neat.

A laconic entry in my Dad's diary the day after the D-Day invasion read:

7th June 1944: Today has been a Red Letter day. Jan took Guinea to the school pet show and won 1st prize and I, playing my 2nd competitive game of Bowls beat Tom Fowler by 22-13.

In class I used to spend some time deep in one of my own books held surreptitiously on my knees out of sight. I realised very quickly that if I "bagged" a desk at the beginning of term in the middle of the room I would be tolerably safe from interference. The 'goodies' sat in the front, eagerly waving their arms in the air to answer questions. The rebels made a line at the back - unless a perspicacious teacher separated them. The middle rows could well be overlooked and I can remember being surprised at looking up and finding myself in the classroom, having been immersed in the adventures of a medieval page called Ferry the Fearless or the orphan Carrots at Orchard End – so much for the "keen little worker" at Newtown House.

This illegal occupation never happened when we were being taught French. Miss Leather was a strict disciplinarian. Tall, with tight gingerish curls and a hawkish eye and usually immersed in a fur coat, she could keep a class in silence even before she left the staff room for the lesson. She brooked no idleness. If she asked a question she would often as not point to a pupil who had not put up her hand. I spent miserable minutes deciding whether it would be less dangerous to raise a hand even though I had no idea of the answer.

I have set myself a time constraint on this saga though I have strayed into later years. I would not want to imply that the High School gave me an indifferent education. On the contrary, in the nine years I spent there the staff did much to interest me in many subjects. The teaching improved, the extra activities, like visits to concerts, operas and plays increased. When Laurence Olivier's film of Henry V came to the cinema in 1944, we were all taken to see it from the juniors to the VIth form. The colour, drama of the speeches, the rousing music of Walton made it an unforgettable experience and kick started a delight in Shakespeare. The school ethos also instilled a sense of responsibility - which has sometimes been a burden – but even if I failed to shine at mathematics and Latin I had a good grounding in everything that was then offered.

For Christmas 1944 an aunt gave me a Charles Letts 1945 Schoolgirl's Diary. It was the first of many diaries that I have written on and off since. This was a small volume, bound in khaki rexine and it was full of worthy information.

First I filled in my name, national registration number, my size in shoes, gloves and hats and my height which was 4'4inches. Then followed a formidable array of facts: the size of sports pitches, British prime Ministers, mathematical formulae and fifteen pages describing careers for women. Clearly the publisher was trying to encourage women to think far beyond Kinder, Küche, and Kirche. I put crosses by all those I did not fancy: Nothing to do with mathematics, science, industry or engineering, though I favoured nursing, teaching and journalism. There were lists of books to read, and ticked were those by Arthur Ransome, Richard Jeffries, Evans *South with Scott,* books of Fairy Tales but no tick beside *301 Things a*

Bright Girl Can Do. French and German verbs were comprehensively listed. "Fancy: German verbs", I said to Mark, my husband, when we were looking at the book. "I expect that was so that you could arrest a parachutist", he quipped, "though there is no verb for 'Surrender!'". Strangest of all to my eyes now was that every week showed a different type of aircraft belonging to all the countries involved in the war and included profiles, horsepower, size, range.

But what of the entries in that first diary? There was only just over an inch of space for each day so I must have decided that Gladstone's third dictum about diaries was the one to follow: "You may take the three proverbial courses about a journal: you may keep none, you may keep a complete and "full-blooded" one, or you may keep a mere skeleton like mine with nothing but bare entries of time and place."

A skeleton it was.

1st January, 1945: *Helped Mummy and played till Dinner. In the Afternoon I went to Grandmas's with Anne & Josie. We played a game had Tea and done some Needlework came home read and went to bed.*

7th January: *Went for a Bike Ride with Daddy. Helped in the shop till dinner played messed about had tea went to bed. Auntie Joan was on leave.*

Did it get better when term started?

18th January: *School! Had Breakfast got on the Bus and went to St Albans to school had Prayers settled in had dinner came home had more dinner done stamps had Tea read and went to bed.*

There could have been a lively entry about catching the bus. The stop was just outside our shop. On many mornings I would rush down the steps from the flat just as the bus drew up. Sometimes my mother would throw something out of the window– like my music case or plimsolls just in time for me to grab them and mount the bus, thanking the patient conductor.

I got tired of the diary very quickly.

28th January: *Not much to say. Went to Butchers and to Grandma.*

That was a Sunday, and "Butchers" was a tobacconist, sweet shop, newsagent. My father used to purchase his Sunday paper and more often than not would buy for me a copy of Arthur Mee's Children's newspaper. I found it somewhat serious and would much have preferred Beano.

14th March: *Got up went to school and you know the rest.*

The next day I stated that I would just put in "special days". There weren't many:

23rd March: *Broke up*
26th March. *Had my report. I was 4th out of 36. Very good*

Note the size of the class. Almost half of the School's pupils had enrolled since the outbreak of war including many from private London schools and many became boarders. The intention had been to add classrooms before 1939 but now there was no money or materials for such work. There were staff shortages too so class numbers were always large.

In April I went to see baby kids at the gamekeeper's house in the Park and the first of May was "a horrible day". I have no idea why. Then nothing. No mention of the end of the war. No description of the festivities. Nothing until:

25th December. *We had a lovely day at Grandma's.*

REAL LOVELY!!!

26th December: *Even better at home.*

Was it all as boring as that? I did mention occasional visits to the pictures, shopping in St Albans and that my cousins came to tea. Those pathetic little entries, badly written and punctuated seem to belie my description of a stable childhood that was full of love and laughter, Took it all for granted I suppose. The quiet fifties; the psychedelic sixties were still to come.

Afterword

Am I carrying my new doll along the road to my grandparent's house, or am I fiercely pressing down the stiff pedals of my new tricycle? No, I am pushing a brown pram containing a new baby brother, because it is 1946 and, although childhood Christmases merge in my memory, this one was special. It was the first Christmas when all the family was together again. We always went to my father's parents at 55 on Christmas Day. I do not suppose that my grandmother asked or demanded, she just assumed that we would be there, be together, laugh, have fun and create family folklore. Which was the Christmas when my new doll cried 'Mamma' in the middle of the King's speech and we girls caught each other's eyes and tried hard not to laugh? Which year did my cousin Anne mischievously hide my tiny white bear so that I, tearfully, had to go home without him?

The preparation even by we children had been intense. Grandma called us in during the week before the feast to make those hideous loops of paper chains which came in strips and gummed on one end were licked and firmly pressed on the other side having been passed through a completed circle. Then there were lengths of paper which spent the years collapsed flat like mini accordions and were satisfyingly pulled out into vivid coloured chains; bells were pulled out into a circle and hung from the stairs. We would be sent up the garden to cut holly and ivy and sprigs would be perched over every picture.

Come the big day thirteen of us were crammed into the dining room for dinner, we three girls at a small table by the French window. The unusual, sumptuous smells of gravy, turkey and Christmas pudding pervaded the room. John, a one year old cousin, cheerfully threw food around the tray of his high-chair. My little brother slept in the hall.

Washing up was done by all the women except Grandma who was sent to sit down with the men. She argued but was always defeated. Grandfather, my father and his two brothers, snoozed in the warm stuffy sitting room, thick with the scent of Grandpa's Nut-brown tobacco and wood smoke from the fire. The washing up had to be finished in time for the King's speech when we all we sat together and listened with respectful attention.

My two cousins, Anne and Josie, and I were, once again, performing a pantomime for the delectation of the adults. After the speech we girls disappeared upstairs to sort out our costumes and Josie and I would get last minute instructions from our draconian producer. This year it was Cinderella. Josie, at eight years old, pretty and cuddly, played the heroine. I, two years older and preferring the male rôle, was the Prince, and Anne, with amazing agility and characterization managed to be two Ugly sisters, mother and Fairy Godmother. She had rare talent – after all, she went on to be a Tiller girl. We younger ones sang to her tune.

Rehearsals had been thorough. We had been meeting since half-term. We would run to our grandmother's at lunchtime or after school. She made tea for us and then we would rehearse in the sitting room, warmed generously by a small portable electric fire. Two years earlier when my grandmother had an American army captain billeted with her we crept into his room one lunch hour, when Gran Tingey was in the garden, rifled the drawers of the dressing table and took a stick of delicious and unobtainable chewing gum. We solemnly divided it into three pieces and chewed it luxuriously on our way back to school.

The dress rehearsal was a weekend engagement. Clothes were brought from our two homes and assessed for suitability. Anne always took the opportunity to wear a proper tutu, used at the displays put on in the village hall by her dancing school. I wore a silver-grey jacket, edged with violet silk, a decorative garment which was part of a wedding outfit worn by a great aunt in the 1900s. My mother had added a foaming lace cravat, black velvet breeches. Grey silk stockings, well-hitched up, completed the costume. I bowed graciously and waved a silk handkerchief, convinced I was indeed the Prince.

On Christmas evening after tea and cake, the adults settled at one end of the room and, while they chatted, my grandmother helped us to prepare the refreshments for the interval. The highlight of this was a large meat plate of small cheese biscuits sandwiching thin slices of turkey. This was placed together with mince pies on the slate shelf in the pantry. Remember, there was still strict rationing.

The play began: The Ugly Sister was beastly, Cinderella cried – not least because she forgot her lines and was hissed at by her sister – and then she had to be urged to cry some more while Anne changed her costume. The coach, a somewhat tame arrangement of two chairs covered by a gold bedspread, got her to the ball, where the Prince bowed and flirted with her and the two danced with grave precision. The slipper was produced and the play was over.

Then came the interval. But what was that? A shriek from Josie in the kitchen where she and Grandma had gone to get the food. Sadly one of us had left the door of the pantry open. "Tibby's eaten the turkey," Josie wailed. Grandma and Anne quickly rearranged the biscuits and the plate was brought in. "Eat them up!" my usually fastidious grandmother commanded the adults. "They won't hurt you."

After that it was the men's turn. They depicted local characters and places and we had to guess what they were. Norman, my large, younger uncle squashed himself into my brother's pram – which was never the same again – wore a bonnet and chewed a dummy. He was supposed to be "Little Pete" who was the child of a somewhat colourful customer at the shop. "What's the weather like, Pete?" one of the assistants would ask the small mite. "Bloody orful!" he would reply with aplomb. He was pushed by Uncle Roly, parading as his mother. "My best hat!" wailed my Gran Hope. And that was never the same again either. Then came a quiz when the audience had to recognize the names of local pubs. Roly went to the back of the sofa, bent down and came slowly up with only his behind showing - in trousers, naturally, for it was 1946 – and he was "The Rising Sun." My father, normally a shy retiring man, was a schoolboy in shorts and a tiny cap stealing apples from old Mr. Murray with the standard lamp acting as the tree. We girls giggled uproariously, delighting to see the grown-ups unbend and play the fool. The end of the entertainment was always the same: my grandmother fortified by a small glass of port would be persuaded to sing 'The Last Rose of Summer', but only if she could stay sitting down.

    The day of warm, simple fun was over for another year. Tweed coats were put on, white party socks and black pumps changed for thick wool socks and sensible brogues, a sleeping baby was slid carefully into his creaking pram and we walked the half mile home. Was there a bright, full moon and frost making the fence tops sparkle? Of course, all Christmas nights were like that.